Proceedings of the 1975 Clinic
on Library Applications
of Data Processing:
The Use of Computers in Literature Searching
and Related Reference Activities in Libraries

Papers presented at the
1975 Clinic on Library Applications
of Data Processing, April 27-30, 1975

The Use Of Computers In Literature Searching And Related Reference Activities In Libraries

Edited by
F. WILFRID LANCASTER

University of Illinois
Graduate School of Library Science
Urbana-Champaign, Illinois

© 1976 by the Board of Trustees of the University of Illinois

LC Card Number: 76-1790
ISBN: 0-87845-043-2
U.S. ISSN: 0069-4789

TABLE OF CONTENTS

INTRODUCTION

The Twelfth Annual Clinic on Library Applications of Data Processing was held at the Ramada Inn, Champaign, Illinois, April 27-30, 1975. The subject of this particular clinic was the application of computers to information retrieval and other aspects of reference service in libraries. An attempt was made, through a combination of formal papers and demonstrations, to cover a wide range of applications of machine-readable data bases in support of the reference activities of libraries. The papers contained in this volume represent a number of different viewpoints and different types of user. Public, academic and industrial libraries are all represented. Some of the papers are presented by consumers, while others are given by retailers of information service.

The paper by Dowlin represents an in-house application of a mini-computer in an information retrieval application, while the paper by Waltz goes beyond citation retrieval and investigates the possibilities of machine systems that might actually answer factual questions posed by library users. Lyon discusses the use of on-line systems in computer-aided instruction in libraries, and the contribution of Schmidmaier reviews the use of machine-readable data bases in Australia. The opening paper and the closing paper are general reviews, the former dealing more with our achievements and the latter with the failures or limitations in the provision of information services.

F. W. LANCASTER
Editor

MARTHA E. WILLIAMS
Director
Information Retrieval Research Laboratory
University of Illinois
Urbana-Champaign

Machine-Readable Data Bases In Libraries: Criteria For Selection And Use

Traditionally, libraries have been the source of stored information—the collective memory of a community or a civilization. In recent years, with the proliferation of publications and governmental involvement in research, machine-readable data bases have evolved as separate entities which store in indexed and abstracted form much of the current information found in libraries. As the quantity of recorded information increases, libraries are, and will be increasingly, forced to rely on these machine-readable data bases to search the accumulated knowledge if they are to retrieve it efficiently—or at all. Some libraries are now providing data base search services to their patrons; many more are considering it.

What is a Data Base?

Data bases are organized collections of information in machine-readable form and exist in almost all of the major fields of science and technology as well as in the social sciences. The collected information may be of several types: bibliographic or bibliographic related, natural-language text, numerical, or representational. An example of a bibliographic data base is the MARC II data base of the Library of Congress, or the Chemical Abstracts Service's (CAS) CA CONDENSATES tapes. CASIA (Chemical Abstracts Subject Index

Alerts) tapes, which contain subject index terms and postings that consist of Chemical Abstracts citation numbers, is an example of a bibliographic-related data base because the citation number refers the user to other tapes or hard-copy sources that contain the full bibliographic citation. A natural-language text data base would be the text portion of the New York Times Information Bank, which contains not the full text of newspaper articles, but textual summaries or abstracts of the articles. System 50 for State Statutes of Aspen Systems Corporation, an example of a full-text data base, contains more than 200 million words of statute law. A familiar example of a numeric data base is the current U.S. census tapes produced by the Bureau of the Census. A data base that contains not alphameric data but graphic or pictorial representations, such as the CAS Registry Structure data base which contains chemical structures, is referred to as a representational data base.

Who Produces Data Bases?

Data bases are produced, or generated, both by governmental sources and by organizations in the private sector. Included in the private sector are profit-making as well as not-for-profit organizations such as professional societies. Although the government is responsible for the generation of numerous data bases, in many cases the actual production work is carried out under contract by either not-for-profit or commercial organizations.

Many of the largest and most heavily used data bases were produced by the federal government, including: the MEDLARS (Medical Literature Analysis and Retrieval System) tapes produced by the National Library of Medicine; the MARC II (Machine-Readable Cataloging) tapes produced by the Library of Congress; the ERIC (Educational Resources Information Center) tapes of the National Institute of Education; the DDC (Defense Documentation Center) tapes of the Department of Defense's Defense Documentation Center; GRA (Government Research Announcements) tapes of the National Technical Information Service (NTIS); and STAR (Scientific and Technical Aerospace Reports) tapes produced by the National Aeronautics and Space Administration. The fact that government-generated data bases are heavily used is a function not only of their usefulness but also of the fact that their production and use are subsidized by the government.

Of the large scientific, technical, and discipline-oriented data bases, many have been produced by professional and technical societies in the not-for-profit part of the private sector. Some of these are: the SPIN (Searchable Physics Information Notices) tapes of the American Institute of Physics; *BA Previews* (Biological Abstracts Previews) of BioSciences Information Service; CA CONDENSATES of Chemical Abstracts Service; PATELL (Psychological Abstracts Tape Edition-Leased or Licensing) of the American

Psychological Association; COMPENDEX (Computerized Engineering Index) of Engineering Index, Inc.; and METADEX (Metals Abstracts Index) of the American Society for Metals. These data bases are produced within the private sector; however, many of them have received research and development funds from the government to help them get started or conduct research associated with systems or products.

The number of profit-making organizations producing data bases is small, but some of these data bases are very important; for example, the Institute for Scientific Information publishes the Science Citation Index (SCI) tapes and the Social Science Citation Index (SSCI) tapes; Excerpta Medica is produced by the Excerpta Medica Foundation; the F & S Index of Corporations and Industries is produced by Predicasts, Inc.; and the New York Times Information Bank is produced by the *New York Times.*

A few data bases were generated specifically for the purpose of information retrieval, but because the cost of data input is high and could seldom be justified for the purposes of retrieval alone, many more were created as by-products of other activities. Some were created because machine-readable data were needed as a component of a computerized-process control or production system for publishing primary journals, indexes or abstracting journals. Others were created as a result of the fact that computerized typesetting was used to produce a hard-copy publication. Computers have proven to be economic and effective tools for producing primary and secondary publications. Consequently, every time a publisher uses computerized photocomposition, a potentially machine-searchable file exists. The machine-readable file, once created, can be automatically reorganized, merged with other machine-readable files, reformatted, and repackaged to meet the demands of various markets. It has become obvious that machine-readable files are considerably more flexible and can serve many more functions than can hard-copy records.

What Kinds of Data Base Services Exist?

Data base services differ in types of service offered and can be classified as either batch mode or on-line, depending on the method chosen to process the information. The different methods of processing are related to the types of service and determine the type of file structure that is best suited to the particular purpose. The basic types of file structure for information retrieval purposes are: (1) inverted, e.g., the alphabetical grouping of terms with postings; and (2) serial, or sequential, in which each record or citation is examined in turn.

An on-line system is one in which the user is in direct communication through a terminal with the central processing unit of the computer. An on-line interactive system is one in which there is literally an interactive two-way communication between the user and the machine, and response by the machine is immediate. On-line searches of bibliographic data bases are usually run against inverted dictionary-type files. On the other hand, a batch processing system is one in which multiple jobs or search questions are "batched" together and run at one time. The search questions can be entered via a terminal, cards or tape; however entered, they are saved until the time of the batch run. Searches against a serially or sequentially arranged file are usually run in the batch mode so that the basic cost of spinning the tape once can be spread over several search questions rather than requiring one question to bear the total cost. There is, of course, some incremental cost for processing the additional questions.

Retrospective and current awareness searches differ with respect to the currentness of the files against which they are processed, and with respect to the number of times the question is run against the files. A retrospective search, or question, is one which is run against older, historical or past files, whereas a current-awareness search is run against only the most recent file. A retrospective question is usually run once against the entire collection of data base issues or volumes, while a current-awareness profile is run many times— each time against the most current issue of the data base. Computerized current-awareness systems are usually called SDI (selective dissemination of information) systems. Information is searched for and retrieved from the file in accordance with a profile of the user's search interests. The output or search results are then disseminated to the user. In the case of SDI, once a profile of the user's interests has been developed and refined, it is run on a regular basis against each new issue of the data bases requested by the user. SDI searches are usually run in the batch mode against sequential files. After an SDI run has been completed on the most current issue, the tape of that issue is added to the retrospective file for its data base. Several of the on-line services now offer SDI in addition to retro-searching. Since they have to process incoming new data base issues as they arrive anyway—in order to add them to the retrospective files—they can conduct the SDI searches at the time of that initial processing. In these cases, search output can either be disseminated to the user through the mail or stored for later retrieval through his terminal. Retrospective questions can be run in either the batch or on-line modes depending on the system on which the search is processed. In most cases the file that is searched is in inverted form for fast searching.

SDI and retrospective searches differ in purpose. The purpose of a retro-search may be to provide the user with: (1) a few relevant references to become acquainted with a topic; (2) a thorough coverage of the literature on a particular subject; or (3) one or more references that contain the answer to a specific question. These searches are conducted on demand and always in "past" or retrospective files. The completeness of the search question processed against the file varies considerably with the user's purpose. In contrast, SDI searches are conducted in order to keep the user up to date with the published literature in his field. The user profile is usually designed to be as complete as possible and to achieve high recall. The same profile is used over and over against new issues of the data base. The profile is modified over the course of a year if changes in user interests or data base output indicate the need. Since SDI and retrospective searches of data bases differ in purpose, comparisons of the two with respect to performance and cost make little sense.

There is another type of service which libraries should be aware of—"private library" service. In this service, the user can have output from any machine search stored for him on a separate disc file along with his own judgments about citations he has received. This feature is now available from several organizations that process data bases. At their own discretion, users may discard unwanted references, add new material, or even augment the file with additional indexing terms for the references already selected. This type of service can be provided on a personal basis or on a company basis. It would be possible, in this way, for a library or a company to generate its own machine-readable files without having to develop its own data base or search strategy.

What Effect Does Data Base Service Have on Library Operations?

Data base searching can have a direct impact on libraries in several ways: (1) it can affect the acquisition policy of the library—either increasing or decreasing acquisitions by pointing out the nonuse of some journals and/or the need for other journals; (2) it can affect the interlibrary loan traffic of the library as either a borrowing organization or as a lending organization, depending on the correspondence between the library's serials and monograph collections and the retrieved citations from data base searches; (3) the library can expand or deepen its services by offering personalized data base search services, for both individuals and organizations, from data bases it processes; (4) the library can function as an intermediary, preparing search questions and processing them via an on-line service, or through another center; or (5) the library can function as a referral center, directing its customers to the appropriate data bases and service centers.

If a library is considering providing data base services to its patrons, it must understand before making a selection what types of services are available, and it must know how to evaluate both data bases and processing centers.

How to Evaluate a Data Base

The potential user of data base services will have to evaluate not only the searching methods available but the content of the data base itself. The subject coverage of data bases may be discipline oriented, mission oriented, problem oriented or multidisciplinary. In evaluating them, a library must first know how their coverage matches the objectives and the breadth of its own collection. Does the data base cover material such as government reports, journal articles, patents, monographs, theses, reprints and news items? If it does, how complete is this coverage? That is, if it claims to cover a particular journal, will it be covered in its entirety or only for selected issues or articles? This information can be hard to find, although many data base producers provide lists of the journals and other items indexed.

Another important consideration is the time lapse between the item's appearance in the primary source, in the secondary source (or index), and finally in the data base. (In some cases a citation appears on a tape before it is produced in a hard-copy secondary source because the hard-copy publication is produced from the tape.)

In addition, one should question the indexing and coding practices. Does the data base include free-language keywords on the tape? Does it include a controlled thesaurus or hierarchical vocabulary terms? Are titles given exactly as the author provided them, or are they augmented titles as in the case of BIOSIS in which additional terminology is added to the author's title? Does it include other kinds of codes to indicate subject matter or any other criteria about the item itself? Are abstracts and extracts available on tape for search and display, or will the library have to go back to the hard copy to obtain them?

The size and growth rate of the data base will indicate something about the number of citations available from one year's accumulation of that file. It is important to know how the tape version corresponds with the hard-copy version. In some cases there is a one-to-one correspondence; that is, for each abstract or reference contained on the hard copy there is a tape representation. In many cases, the data base itself is a subset of the hard-copy version; or the reverse may be true, i.e., the data base may contain more citations than the hard copy. In other cases, such as the MARC tapes from the Library of Congress, there is no corresponding hard-copy publication (except the collection of LC cards). If there is a corresponding hard copy, a library can occasionally do both computer and manual searches of an issue as a cross-check to be sure it is using the right terminology and really getting what is wanted.

Important Concerns for Library Internal Data Base Processing

As a processor, the library must investigate the consistency and quality control exercised by the data base supplier, and must also be aware of the frequency with which changes are made in the data base and in the provisions for notification to the processor of data base changes. If the supplier indicates forenames of authors by first initials and later decides to use full first names instead, this of course affects processing. Addition of new data elements affects processing time as well, and possibly requires a change in the search program. Adherence to a delivery schedule is another concern of the processor. If the data base supplier sends his tapes late, then the library will be delayed in providing output to its clients.

There is another consideration in looking at data bases: If the library plans to use more than one data base, is there overlap of subject coverage between them? There are costs associated with intellectual processing (indexing and abstracting) and manual inputting of citations. If the same citation is handled more than once, this can represent wasted time, effort and money. The processor also wastes money by having to search for the same material on more than one set of tapes. There are a few processing centers that merge several data bases to create one common data base. This is being done at Ohio State University and for the pollution data base (Pollution Information Program—PIP) at the National Science Library in Canada, but in general most centers search each data base as an individual entity.

A final—and much more technical—processing concern is that of compatibility between various data bases. The variability among the data bases complicates handling for those who process them. The standard arrangement of data element tags, data content, and directory information for the records is referred to as the format of the record, and the arrangement of the records on a tape or other media is referred to as the file structure or file format.

Unfortunately, file formats and record formats are not standardized, nor are the definitions, contents and representations of the data elements. There are almost as many data base formats as there are data bases, which leads to confusion and, of course, added expense in processing tapes, because it requires the processor of multiple tapes to either develop multiple search programs or to reformat all incoming tapes to one standard format. One important standard has been developed by the American National Standards Institute for interchange or transmittal of bibliographic records: the "American National Standard for Bibliographic Information Interchange on Magnetic Tape." The MARC implementation of this standard has been proposed as a Federal Information Processing Standard and, barring problems, it will go into effect as a federal standard. This standard deals only with the format for records on tape or the generalized structure, not with the contents of the records. It does not define data elements or tags, specify required data elements, or specify data representation beyond that of the required character set.

Important Concerns for Library External Data Base Processing: How to Evaluate Processing Centers

The processing of data bases is an expensive activity and most libraries will be interested in buying these services from an information center. There are a number of questions the library will need to ask itself, and ask each center under consideration, when evaluating the relative merits of the many centers available.

Some of these questions are: Does a center have the data base or mix of data bases that will satisfy the needs of the library's clientele? When the appropriate mix of data bases has been found, does the processing center retain all the records from each of the data bases the library is using, or does it strip off certain parts of some of the tapes? It is essential to know whether or not all of the information in a data base is being searched. Does the center employ a standard internal format? Will all data bases be processed the same way? Will all of the output received by the library look (be formatted) the same?

Does the center provide any kind of document backup? Most centers do not because of the cost associated with resource location and acquisition. The Institute for Scientific Information (ISI), however, provides document backup for anything that is in their *Current Contents* through Lockheed's DIALOG and System Development Corporation's ORBIT on-line systems. Anyone searching ISI tapes on these systems can enter a request for a document. The requests are saved by the systems and transmitted back to Philadelphia every night. Documents are mailed out the following day. A similar system is available for the National Technical Information Service (NTIS) tapes. The Ohio State University's Mechanized Information Center (MIC) system also provides document delivery from its own collections.

There are other services which some centers provide: off- or on-site training for library personnel; manuals to assist users in writing profiles and search strategies; free demonstration searches to give an idea of system capability; dictionaries, vocabulary lists or thesauri for controlled vocabulary; term frequency lists for title terms; and free-language keywords. It is important to ascertain whether the revision of search profiles is permitted and whether this imposes an added cost. Some centers supply a newsletter to keep users informed about changes in indexing practices or the addition of new data elements, so that they can modify their search strategies to accommodate such changes. In some instances provision is made for feedback or data base monitoring, to aid in calculating the precision rating for searches. All these things relate to the general cooperativeness of the center staff and their accessibility to the patron.

The data elements provided in the output are of special interest to the client or patron. Which elements are included in the actual printout or display? Are just the title and the author name shown, or also the keywords? Are the terms in the search which caused this particular item to be a "hit" shown? How are the data elements arranged on the output medium? How many citations are there per page? If large computer paper is used, are the citations printed in two adjacent columns so that the paper can be cut into two file-size portions? Are there options available for sorting the output? For example, can one specify that the output be sorted alphabetically by author's name, numerically by reference number, in descending order according to ranked weight or value, or by date of publication? Will the output from different data bases be displayed in a standard format for easy visual scanning? Will both upper and lower case characters be used? All of these features may be of considerable importance to a library and to its clientele.

External Processing: Search Output Options

Some centers display retrieved information on cathode ray tubes (CRTs), in which case the user is likely to require that paper copy, or hard copy, also be printed off-line and sent to him. On request, some centers can generate microform output directly from the tape. The output can also be supplied on magnetic tape itself for later in-house use. Most suppliers require, however, that the output be provided on hard copy, both to avoid copyright difficulties and to provide records of the citations retrieved for the purposes of reimbursing the supplier with appropriate royalties.

Assuming that the output is provided on hard copy, there are still many possibilities from which to choose. For instance, some centers can produce output on multilith masters for further reproduction. (This feature could be especially useful to libraries, for example, in the production of SDI bibliographies or bulletins.) The output can be on cards or on computer paper of various sizes. If it is on cards, it will be easily separable into unit records; false hits can then be discarded and pertinent citations interfiled with other material in a constantly updated card file. If output is on computer printout paper, the whole group of citations may have to be retained or the desired references cut out of the pages.

External Processing: Search Features to Look For

When evaluating the search capability of a particular center, it is important to ask which information items or data elements are routinely searched. Data elements are the basic building blocks of data bases. In the case of bibliographic data bases, some of the commonly searched data elements are: author, title, journal name, volume number, issue number, date of publication, index term, keyword, and publisher name. The data element is the smallest unit or element within an information or data field which contains one or more data elements. Usually multiple data elements and fields make up a bibliographic record. A record is the representation on magnetic tape of the physical book or article, etc., in much the same way that a card in the library card catalog represents the book on the shelf. Records, in turn, comprise a file. Ordinarily one file makes up a data base, but sometimes a data base contains several files.

A searcher should be permitted to access both individual records within a file, and individual data elements (fields) within individual records. Thus, in formulating a search question or request, the searcher should be able to specify certain search terms or data elements; the computer should search the index portion of each record in the data base to locate search term or data element matches, and then produce a printout or CRT display of the records that contain those matches. On the other hand, if the searcher knows the citation or reference number of certain desired records, he should be able to specify these directly and have the matching records printed or displayed immediately.

It is possible to search specified data elements within an individual record either because the elements are identified by unique codes, or because the position of an element within a record may specify what type of element it is. Often a directory is associated with each record which specifies the elements that are present, their location in the record, and the length (number of alphameric characters) of the data content.

There is a difference between the data elements used in searching and those displayed in output. Searchable elements are often a subset of those displayed. Abstracts, for instance, are seldom searched but often displayed. Abstracts provide sufficient contextual information to the user to aid him in determining whether he has a "hit," i.e., whether or not the terms in his search have succeeded in locating an article he needs. In some cases abstracts themselves may be searched, but this is seldom done because it significantly increases search time and cost, usually with little added benefit. The number of access points, or searchable data elements, greatly influences system ability to achieve high recall and precision in searching. Some centers only permit searches on subject terminology, i.e., words found in the title, keywords, or index terms. Others permit searches on author, company affiliation, LC class number or Dewey Decimal number, report numbers of various types, languages, countries of origin, or other types of data elements. (Obviously, some data elements are specific to certain data bases, e.g., Engineering Index card-a-lert codes are found only in COMPENDEX.) It is important to ask whether, as in the case of MEDLINE, hierarchical terms can be used in searching, and, whether there is a way to distinguish among the data elements—e.g., can an author word be distinguished from a subject term? This last distinction is important in order to avoid retrieving false hits due to homographs.

What kind of logic is permitted in search strategies? Is full Boolean logic permitted (using *and, or*, and *not* operators), or are there restrictions? Some centers provide adjacency logic, i.e., they permit specification of the context in which a term occurs. For example, the searcher can indicate that a term must occur within one or two words of another term as opposed to being found anywhere in the record. This feature is available in several systems.

Another feature to look for is the availability of truncation, which is the ability to search on a fraction of a term. For example, a user interested in the concept *analysis* can include in his search question the term fraction *analy** (truncating after the y), and thereby retrieve all occurrences of the terms analysis, analytical, analytics, etc. Without this feature, it would be necessary to specify all the variant forms of a word that an author may have used. Title terms, in most data bases, are not generated from a controlled vocabulary but contain natural-language, or freely generated, terms. The searcher must then be able to adjust to the term variability provided. Most centers provide right truncation only; however, left truncation can be extremely useful. For example, if a person was interested in antibiotics and searched under the term fraction **mycin*, he would hit approximately forty different variations of that term, which is probably more than he would have been able to think of easily. The limit to the number of characters that can be truncated must be established, and it must be decided whether truncation is available for term types other than subject words. Another important question about searching is whether or not the system can provide ranges for numeric data. Could one search for items published between 1972 and 1975 only, for example? And finally, in the case of on-line systems, is there the capability for one to review search strategy, or to save search strategies for later use? Can the system answer inquiries about system operation, e.g., explain commands and responses, and are the explanations available at several levels of sophistication? New features are constantly being added to on-line systems; one must keep up to date with them in order to make effective use of the tools provided.

External Processing: Comparing and Evaluating Processing Center Costs

Cost features, although often considered first, should be secondary considerations after the selection of the appropriate data bases and centers that provide suitable searching and output features. Generally, costs are competitive and do not vary much.

Charges can be established in several ways. Does a center charge an annual fee? Does it charge for profile writing? Is there a charge for the number of terms used in a search, or is some maximum number of terms allowed and then an assessment made when this number is exceeded? Does the center charge on the basis of the number of hits received in the searching, or is a maximum established and a charge levied only after the maximum is reached? Is there an additional charge for postage, user aids, or for the media on which the output is received? If an on-line system is being used, are charges based on connect time, terminal use, or hard-copy output? Some systems have different fees for different types of search terms which are based on the frequency with which a term occurs. A high-frequency term costs more to search than a low-frequency term.

Should a base fee be charged for the service? There are several organizations which charge a base fee within which one can charge various kinds of services, each associated with a certain number of units. For example, an SDI profile might cost five units per year, and a retrospective search two units per volume. A library could, for example, buy a package of 100 units and then use them in any desired manner.

There are many different ways to charge users. The purchaser must become thoroughly familiar with the charge or fee bases of the particular centers he is interested in, in order to compare services effectively.

Evaluating Your Organization

In looking at your own position with respect to adding data base services, there are a number of areas to consider:

1. *Need*—How does the proposed computerized data base search service fit with and add to current service to meet further the needs of your own organization? You know what services are already available and what your users will and will not accept.

2. *Staff*—How are you going to handle increased demand for service? If the new service becomes very popular, will this mean the acquisition of new staff? Furthermore, the provision of computerized search services usually affects staff assignments, especially if many people were previously involved in manual current-awareness or retrospective searching. In most cases, the real effect of instituting computerized search service is that many more searches get done. Staff training and support is an additional consideration.

3. *Hard-copy backup*—How will this new service affect your journal acquisition policy? It may tell you that you cannot provide from your own collection adequate document backup for your users. It may point out that some of your journals are never used, or seldom produce useful hits. (Obviously, there are some journals that are not included by the indexing services, which does not necessarily mean that they are of no value to you.) It may indicate journals that should be added to the collection or for which multiple copies are needed. In any event, the new service almost certainly will have an impact on your journal acquisition policy. Often, the introduction of computer-based information retrieval services also has an impact on interlibrary loan activities.

4. *Cost justification*—You will probably have to justify the cost of the new service to your own management. What is the difference between the old searching methods and the new method? What is the ability of your staff to "sell" the services in-house? Often, the new service will have to be introduced to people who have never heard of computer-based retrieval systems before. If you want to provide a service, you will have to be prepared to justify its cost explicitly.

5. *Who pays for it*—How are these services usually financed? In some organizations, an individual user will actually pay for his own services, but this is by far the least popular method. In some cases the service is purchased through a library budget; in others, through a departmental budget. Specific projects, grants or contracts may pay for the services used. In some cases the overhead of the total organization pays for them. You know your organization, and you know which is the most likely source of funds.

6. *Feedback and evaluation*—How will you handle the feedback and evaluation of this service? Feedback regarding coverage, cost, turnaround time, and especially user satisfaction, can be very helpful. You will have to keep records to evaluate the successes and failures of the service, in order to be able, at the end of the first year, to justify its continuation for another year.

In general, libraries do choose to have data processing done by outside centers. In a library setting, the patron or end-user is not usually the person who writes the search profile or operates the system, even in the case of on-line systems. Searches are usually delegated to information specialists or reference librarians. Cost benefits and effective information retrieval go hand in hand with searching expertise, i.e., searches done by someone who is up to date with data base and system changes, with center services, and especially with the command languages of on-line systems.

These are just a few of the considerations involved in the acquisition of data base services. The questions that are appropriate to you will depend on your own organization, its accounting system, and its service orientation, but it is essential that the questions presented here be among those asked.

Portions of this paper are included in two papers by the author: "The Impact of Machine-Readable Data Bases in Library and Information Services," prepared for the National Commission on Libraries and Information Science, April 1975; and "Criteria for Evaluation and Selection of Data Bases and Data Base Services," *Special Libraries* 66:561-69, Dec. 1975.

BIBLIOGRAPHY

Brandhorst, W. T., and Williams, Martha. "Data Bases: A Review of the Reviews," *Bulletin of the American Society for Information Science* 1:21-22, June-July 1974.

Keenan, Stella, ed. *Key Papers on the Use of Computer-Based Bibliographic Services*. Washington, D. C., American Society for Information Science and National Federation of Abstracting and Indexing Services, 1973.

Lancaster, F. W., and Fayen, E. G. *Information Retrieval: On-Line*. Los Angeles, Melville, 1973.

Marron, Beatrice, *et al. A Study of Six University Based Information Systems* (NBS Technical Note 781). Washington, D. C., National Bureau of Standards, June 1973.

Mauerhoff, Georg R. "Selective Dissemination of Information." *In* Melvin J. Voigt, ed. *Advances in Librarianship*. Vol. 4. New York, Academic Press, 1974, pp. 25-62.

Schneider, John H., *et al.*, eds. *Survey of Commercially Available Computer-Readable Bibliographic Data Bases*. Washington, D. C., American Society for Information Science, 1973.

Williams, Martha E. "Use of Machine-Readable Data Bases." *In* Carlos A. Cuadra and Ann W. Luke, eds. *Annual Review of Information Science and Technology*. Vol. 9. Washington, D. C., American Society for Information Science, 1974, pp. 221-84.

Williams, Martha E., and Stewart, Alan K. *ASIDIC Survey of Information Center Services*. Chicago, IIT Research Institute, 1972.

SALLY BACHELDER
Marketing Representative
The New York Times Information Bank
New York, New York

The New York Times Information Bank: A User's Perspective

The New York Times Information Bank, developed by the *New York Times*, is a computerized, interactive information storage and retrieval system designed to provide easy and efficient access to more than sixty different current events publications. The Information Bank has been developed with the end user specifically in mind; every effort has been made to bridge the gap between the world of automated information systems and the student, business executive, government official or other information seeker. The kind of information the system offers, covering a wide variety of current events topics that address a large and diverse audience, demands that the Information Bank be an easy-to-operate tool, readily available to the end user.

The New York Times Information Bank has been under active development since mid-1966, although it had been extensively discussed prior to that time. In January 1968, the *Times Index* began computer-assisted production. While all the indexing and abstracting of the *New York Times* continues to be done by human indexers, many of the time-consuming clerical and production functions were taken over by the computer.[1] With the *New York Times* in machine-readable form, the next step was to develop a method for the computer to tap this vast information resource selectively. Systems design was a cooperative effort of the *Times* while formal systems analysis and programming were performed by IBM's Federal Systems Division.

In January 1973, the first Information Bank installation was operating in the Hillman Library of the University of Pittsburgh. An active marketing program soon began, and the Information Bank presently has more than seventy subscribers in the United States, Canada and Mexico.

At this writing, the Information Bank's six-year data base consists of almost one million items drawn from more than sixty different sources. Virtually 100 percent of the information content of the *New York Times* is included, as well as selected articles from other newspapers and journals published in the United States and abroad, such as the *Washington Post*, the *Los Angeles Times*, the *Wall Street Journal, Business Week, Time, Newsweek,* and the *London Sunday Times*. The data base consists of 54.8 percent U.S. newspapers, 23 percent special-interest journals, 13.1 percent overseas publications, and 9.1 percent U.S. general-interest magazines. It is updated daily, with approximately 20,000 items coming on-line monthly. Most material is current to within six weeks of publication, while *New York Times* material is available four working days after publication.

A typical Information Bank installation consists of a cathode ray tube (CRT) computer terminal (used for querying the data base), an attached hard-copy printer, a telephone data set or acoustic coupler and, optionally, a microfiche (or microfilm) reader/printer. The search is developed interactively via the CRT, copies are made of the relevant journal abstracts retrieved, and full texts of desired articles are viewed or printed from fiche or film.

A basic Information Bank inquiry can be accomplished in four steps:

1. *Term entry* This is the point where the operator enters the research question in the form of search terms. There are four basic term types: personal name, organization name, geographic location, and subject. (To aid the searcher with subject terms, the Information Bank provides a two-volume printed thesaurus of descriptors, an on-line thesaurus and a subject authority list.)

2. *Modification* At this step the searcher may impose any number of bibliographic or content modifications on the search to obtain greater output relevance. The searcher may limit his response by date, journal, illustration, type of material, news, paper section or page, etc.

3. *Logic* In this final step the searcher combines the files he/she has selected using the full complement of Boolean connectives: *and, or, not.*

4. *Abstract viewing* The searcher may now review the output. An average Information Bank search (to be discussed in greater detail later in this paper) takes approximately fourteen minutes.

The wide range of current subscribers attests to the Information Bank's flexibility and diversity of application. Many public libraries and universities are actively using the Information Bank—including Free Library of Phila-delphia, Connecticut State Library, Kansas City Public Library, Adelphi University, and the University of California at Berkeley and at Los Angeles—and represent one segment of the user population. They utilize the Infor-mation Bank primarily for reference needs: to provide current facts as well as in-depth analyses and surveys of current events, topics of current concern, etc. The largest group of subscribers is the corporate, including such organizations as Coca-Cola, B.F. Goodrich, American Express, Exxon, Hill and Knowlton, Chase Manhattan Bank and General Foods. These subscribers use the Infor-mation Bank to keep up with state and federal legislation that affects them and their industry, to monitor thier competitors, to review foreign affairs as they interact with their own interests, and to aid them in personnel develop-ment and labor concerns. A number of government agencies are finding the Information Bank to be a valuable research tool; installations can be found at the State Department, the Library of Congress, the Central Intelligence Agency, the National Bureau of Standards, and both houses of Congress. Their applications directly relate to the information interests of the department supporting the installation.

As the title of this paper suggests, my discussion of the New York Times Information Bank is going to come from its subscribers' points of view. Often, more can be learned about an on-line information system by under-standing the operational methods of present users than by an extended discussion of the system's capabilities. I intend to "walk around to the other side of the desk," and share some of the problems, concerns and general impressions I have received from our large and diverse group of subscribers. I have no experimental results to present, only the impressions I have received over the past two and one-half years, first as a subscriber, then as an Information Bank customer service representative, and now as a marketing representative. Simply, my comments will fall into three areas: those relating to the day-to-day operation of the system, to its cost considerations, and to its management concerns.

FACTORS AFFECTING DAILY OPERATIONAL CONCERNS

Learning to live with an automated information system can be a joy forever or a perennial problem, depending on the amount of planning that precedes an installation and daily sustains it. One of the first questions that our subscribers face is: Where should we put our CRT? There is a very definite relationship between hardware placement and resource utilization. Much time, money and effort go into the design of a new library; as professionals who analyze work flow and develop proper space utilization to suit the needs of a library and its patrons, library architects are in demand.

Why then, are these principles largely overlooked when a CRT is being installed? A number of subscribers place their terminals in a given area because, for example, an empty table is there, that space is not presently used, or they do not want to rearrange existing equipment. Since placement is so important, these should not be the major decisive factors. One should rather ask: Who is going to use the system the most? The answer should help to determine placement. Is the public relations department going to be the heaviest user? Should they have the terminal? Can we put the terminal by the reference desk in the library, or must it be in a special "data services" area? Should the unit be visible, or should it be hidden?

The major portion of our corporate subscribers have installed the Information Bank in their corporate information centers, or in business libraries. Half as many have placed the terminal in the public relations department or the public relations library, and a small group have placed the system in their marketing divisions. The system usually has been the responsibility of the business, public relations or marketing librarian or researcher. There are some exceptions to this: one terminal has been installed in a personnel department, two others in technical information centers, one in a company president's office, and another in a room by itself. Low usage levels indicate that these latter locations have hampered system access. Incorrect placement puts constraints on the user and thereby prevents full utilization.

All of our public library, college and university subscribers have the Information Bank in their main, or central, library buildings. They are evenly divided concerning terminal placement: an equal number of systems are installed at the reference desk as are installed in a special area devoted to the system. Two subscribers have the system in the telephone reference area, one in the periodicals area, and one in the special law library.

The reason for placing the terminal at the reference desk is obvious: the Information Bank is an excellent reference tool. The majority of our library subscribers turn to the Information Bank many times each day; with the bank at the desk, it is readily available to supply the information required to answer questions. Usually the system is used when either it is the only source that will supply the information, or when the time required for a manual search is so great as to be prohibitive. The bank is used to provide, for example, book and theater reviews, analyses of topics of current interest, information on state and federal legislators, information on the environment, and information on the economy. The bank is not used to answer a "how many" question (How many tons of coal were dug in Kentucky in 1974?), but rather to answer to "tell me about' question (What effect is the coal industry having on Kentucky?). The bank is not used for developing scholarly bibliographies, but for providing topical information.

Some libraries do not put the terminal at the reference desk, but set it aside in its own area. The reasons for doing this incorporate many of the attitudes taken by the library management toward the Information Bank. Some have established special "data services" centers, apart from the general reference desk, that contain (or will contain) all the automated information systems. Such a center normally demands a full-time staff, and becomes an additional link in the reference chain that can either strengthen or weaken the reference services offered. Some subscribers choose to keep the system away from the reference desk because of the obvious visibility of the terminal and the system. This leads to another concern: Should the terminal be displayed?

Overall, no consensus has been reached. Advocates of open and visible placement say that it stimulates interest in the library and its services, makes it easy for the librarian to run searches quickly, permits easy interaction between searcher and patron to allow for rapid relevance judgments, and generally helps to assure good resource utilization. Opponents maintain that the terminal should not be visible because it inspires "curiosity" searches that are time- and money-consuming, places the hardware in a potentially hazardous position, and prevents the librarian or researcher running the system from adequately covering the reference desk.

As the success of the system depends upon easy access and maximum utilization, these two basic decisions—where the terminal is to be located and whether it should be visible to the patron—are key decisions and should be carefully considered before installation.

Equally important is the allocation of staff for the operation of the system. Should the patron operate the terminal? Does the librarian conduct the entire search, or portions of it? Who should be trained in system operation? Who should not? How many people need to be trained? As I have mentioned before, the Information Bank is designed with the end user in mind. All instructions for operating the system appear on the CRT screen; it is not necessary to digest a thick instruction manual. In addition, the structure of an Information Bank inquiry never varies, so the infrequent user can easily navigate the search process. By using conversational English and avoiding all function keys, the Information Bank is a simple system to master.

Nonetheless, the vast majority of our subscribers designate certain staff members as system operators, and do not have a large flow of users tapping into the system. There are two reasons for this. First, knowledge and familiarity with our controlled vocabulary come with experience and sustained usage. While we have over 400,000 different index terms, and people, company or geographic location searches are easy, efficient subject searching is enhanced by an understanding of the subject vocabulary. While an infrequent user can enter a name or place quite easily, a subject can be more difficult. Second, an infrequent user is a slower system operator than a frequent user; as with all other things, time is money. Although it is possible for the end user to query the data base, costs are keeping him away. While today's technology has made the Information Bank and its user orientation possible, today's economy is preventing the user from gaining full control of the inquiry process.

Two choices are therefore available: the library can allow the user to use the system once the abstract viewing stage is reached, or it can keep the user away from all aspects of the system operation. Presently, the majority of our subscribers take the latter approach. It is the librarian or researcher who operates the system. While there are exceptions to this (IBM Armonk, Hill and Knowlton, Defense Intelligence Agency, Army War College), they represent a small percentage. One reason for this, in addition to the ones stated above is, that the business executive or government official does not have the time to operate the Information Bank. He/she has researchers on the payroll, and they are utilized. The executive or official wants the information, not the system. Also, library telephone reference services pervent the user from gaining hands-on access, as does placement of the terminal in a separate room or an out-of-the-way area.

The Information Bank suggests that subscribers create a core user group of four or five people who have sole responsibility for system operation. Training by Information Bank representatives can be easily accomplished for a group of this size in a day or two. Such a group is large enough so the system can always be "covered" by someone, yet small enough to allow each operator to spend enough time on the system to gain expertise. In a library, these operators should be drawn from the reference area; in the corporate sphere, they should be drawn from a centrally located information center in order to permit the entire company to call on them. A good supplement to this, as practiced by the State Department, is to have members of each interested department be Information Bank "representatives," and to have them coordinate departmental information needs with the core operator group. Libraries also practice this approach. It is important to establish and strengthen ties between the reference desk (or data services office) and the other library centers to avoid wasting time and money. For example, one librarian, not fully aware of her institution's use of the Information Bank, worked on a question for four hours, and retrieved one item. When it was suggested that the bank be utilized, forty-six citations were retrieved in twénty minutes.

Once the terminal has been placed and an ample number of operators designated, some projections should be made concerning expected system usage levels to insure proper work scheduling. This is a very difficult matter for most of our subscribers. The Information Bank is such a unique resource that they have no prior experiences on which to draw. For this reason, the Information Bank permits new subscribers, for a 30-day period, to use up to

	College and University	Public Library	Corporate	Government
Mean	27.7 hrs.	23.2 hrs.	15.6 hrs.	32.4 hrs.
Median	25	21	15	18
Modal range	25-34	11-15	7-18	7-18
Absolute range	3-66	10-49	0-71	1-102

Table 1. Monthly System Usage Levels

200 hours of system access time while paying for only 12 hours. This "free" start-up period is designed to allow system experimentation and a lot of system practice prior to the beginning of regular service. During this time subscribers should monitor usage carefully to enable them to anticipate future usage levels and plan accordingly. Normally, usage is very high during that first month: as much as ninety-two hours of usage time is not uncommon. The second month witnesses a drop from the previous month's level as subscribers begin paying for all of their time. Then, slowly, the monthly usage level rises as the institution becomes more familiar with the resource. This rise continues until the library reaches its own "natural level." Incorporation of the bank into the daily reference routine, greater search sophistication on the part of the operators, and an increased awareness of the limits of the system all contribute to this "natural level." Table 1 outlines monthly system usage levels for our present subscribers, broken down by type.

Based on a small sample taken from each subscriber type, the following average duration of a single system operation has been drawn: high—23.9 minutes, low—5.8 minutes, median—14.1 minutes, mean—13.3 minutes. These figures have been created by adding the total number of minutes used by thirteen different subscribers over a three-month period and dividing by the number of searches run. Generally, but not absolutely, one could say that these figures represent an average inquiry length; it is possible for subscribers to run more than one search at a time, and to "batch" inquiries. A rough statement may be made, however: a complete Information Bank inquiry can take anywhere from eight to eighteen minutes. Factors (besides operator expertise) affecting the amount of on-line time are: (1) number of times the on-line thesaurus is referenced, (2) number of files accessed, (3) number of citations retrieved, (4) number of prints taken, and (5) number of times the question is restated and rerun.

Some basic conclusions about Information Bank usage may be drawn from these figures and from our billing records. The Information Bank is a resource that is tapped frequently for relatively short periods of time. It is accessed when the question demands, and the system seems to be fulfilling its goal of providing information efficiently on demand. It is not a resource that is used to compile bibliographies once or twice a week, but a system that provides facts, figures and surveys throughout the day.

As mentioned earlier, what are retrieved from the Information Bank are informative abstracts of relevant articles or journal essays. A factor affecting the day-to-day operation of the system, therefore, is the demand which the system places on microform collections of the full texts. How often is the source article referenced? If the library holds that periodical, what is the additional demand on the collection? If it does not, what is the additional demand on interlibrary loan? Unfortunately, we have no way of monitoring this aspect of system operation. I have been given one set of statistics on this matter, however, by the Connecticut State Library.[2] Over a nine-month period, its Library Line telephone reference service took 624 abstracts prints and 119 full-text prints. They subscribe to the *New York Times* on micro-fiche, as do 62 percent of our subscribers. The fiche, with its compact size and speed of retrieval, is an ideal complement to the Information Bank. In most cases, the fiche collection is placed next to the terminal, thereby creating a "one-step" information area. Our other subscribers either rely on the micro-film collections they already had, or have made their own arrangements.

COST CONSIDERATIONS

The cost of an Information Bank installation falls into three categories: hardware, communications and access time. The system is compatible with a number of different CRTs, and their monthly rental costs range from $98 to $193. If an organization already has a compatible unit, it may be used at no additional cost. It is necessary to establish a telephone connection between the subscribing institution and New York; this entails telephone line charges and modem rentals. If a WATS band or other bulk telephone facility is available, it may be used. The final cost area is Information Bank access, which is based on a transactional schedule: the institution pays just for the amount of time that it uses. The fee is based on computer connect time, or the time elapsed between sign-on and sign-off. The cost per minute is eighty-three cents if you are accessing the bank at 1200 baud, and ninety cents if access is at 2000 or 2400 baud, with a minimum service level of four hours per month.

Returning to our "average" Information Bank inquiry, we can see that a typical search may cost the subscriber from $6.64 to $14.94 for system access. To determine the full cost, telephone charges, hardware costs and staff time costs must be added. All these additional charges vary greatly from subscriber to subscriber, and no real average total cost per inquiry can be developed. It is up to the subscriber, during the one-month start-up period, to determine his own individual costs. Overall, a subscribing institution, after obtaining the necessary hardware and telephone facilities, may expect to spend from $12,000 to $15,000 annually for full Information Bank service.

The manner in which this cost is handled varies from subscriber to subscriber. Basically, four funding strategies have emerged. The most direct method is to take the funds directly out of the library or departmental budget. An alternative has been to seek special funding outside of the budget. This is a more difficult way to proceed, because special funds have a way of drying up, leaving existing programs stranded. A third method is to obtain support for the installation from more than one source. A prime example of this approach can be found at the University of California at Berkeley. Realizing the many applications of the system, the library petitioned those departments within the university for whom the Information Bank could have direct application, requesting from each a small amount of funding to enable the library to offer the service. With their support, the Information Bank was placed on campus. The cost for service beyond the level funded by the departments is to be assumed by the library.[3] Similar approaches can be found among corporate subscribers.

A fourth approach is to make the installation self-sustaining, and charge for service. I will not discuss the very large problem of how one charges for information: e.g., by the number of articles retrieved, by the number of prints made, by the total amount of time spent, by the number of inquiries made. Do you charge back the entire cost, or do you assume a portion of it? If the latter, what percentage do you absorb? Suppose an automated search is not specifically requested by the patron, but the librarian chooses to use the tool; do you charge or not? If not, how do you deal with a question designed specifically for the tool, thereby implying (although not demanding) that an automated search be run?

While many of our subscribers are seriously considering or have considered charging for Information Bank service, less than 5 percent of our present subscribers do so. This small percentage attests to the difficulty of the problem. On April 15, 1975, FIND/SVP, a worldwide information network that retails information services to a large number of subscribers, began offering Information Bank service. They intend to charge the patron with the total cost of the search as well as a standard commercial markup. Factors affecting the total price will be the patron's status (Are they subscribers, or is this a one-time request?) as well as the number of abstracts retrieved. In time, a standard charging policy will be developed based on their initial experiences.[4] At this time, however, I have nothing definitive to report on the subject.

These last two funding methods (multiple funding sources and charging for individual searches) reflect a different attitude toward an Information

Bank installation than the first two (the host department absorbing the entire cost or finding special funding) seem to reflect. These two distinct attitudes can be summed up as: (1) the Information Bank is a special service, different from all that has gone before, and (2) it is simply a computerized extension of the existing reference tools. Either the Information Bank is a big event for an institution, a step into the future, or it is merely the application of modern technology to functions and services that have already been provided. It is acknowledged that the computer allows greater service than ever before, but this new service level can be seen as the "average" service level that a progressive information center should expect to maintain in the years ahead.

To view the Information Bank as just another, albeit more modern, library tool is to believe that the support of this tool should come from the library budget or from special library funds. It is an acquisition of the library and its maintenance is the responsibility of the library. In the past the library has been given a budget to provide information service, and future budgets should provide for future information services.

While I agree that the use of the computer for information retrieval does not create a research tool that is a strange new hybrid, the cost of such an application does demand that the tool be viewed in a unique light. Until either system costs come down or library budgets increase, a computerized information storage and retrieval system should be viewed as a special tool, and no single department should be expected to fund it. While the librarian and researcher should view the Information Bank as simply an extension of their present resources, the management should view it as a resource requiring special attention. I personally feel that support drawn from all quarters of the institution is the most stable and therefore the best way for a subscriber to proceed. By sharing the costs, service can be provided to all. Financial commitment to the system by each department helps to insure maximum utilization by each department and, therefore, full information service to each department. Of course if funds exist within the information center's budget, they should be taken advantage of; if not, service should not be denied the organization because of a tight information center budget, especially since the Information Bank is designed for easy use by the whole organization.

MANAGEMENT CONCERNS

A discussion of cost considerations most naturally leads to a discussion of other, more general management concerns. If the information center decides to make the Information Bank "financially visible" to the organization, it must be concerned with the problems of system promotion. To date, our subscribers have taken various avenues of approach to this. Dentsu Advertising held a large press conference for the Japanese press to develop interest among that firm's clientele. Exxon Corporation held management seminars designed to introduce the Information Bank to the company and reintroduce the business library and all of its services. Basically, the Information Bank was used as a "drawing card" for the executive management. Travelers Insurance Company held similar sessions, and also discovered the public relations value such a new tool has for the library. The success of these meetings can be seen in the increased system utilization they experienced. The Kansas City (Missouri) Public Library has invited a number of library, city and state officials to view the Information Bank and the other projects under active development there. Such "open houses" do much for library public relations.

Some of our subscribers have chosen to go outside of their own organizations for support. Adelphi University is going to hold two "early bird" system demonstrations for prominent Long Island businessmen in an effort to elicit inquiries and therefore financial support. Connecticut State Library had a press conference and reception to introduce the Information Bank to the state, and also to help advertise the state's "Library Line," a statewide information service the bank supports. If financial support is sought outside of the library or information center's budget, or if a budgetary increase is requested for Information Bank service, such system promotion is essential.

For those libraries that are independently absorbing Information Bank costs, system promotion has been avoided. In many cases, just as the system has remained "financially invisible" to the organization, so too has the terminal been "invisible" to the patron. Outside of the library, the university or corporation does not know the Information Bank is available and, when searches are run to serve their information needs, the source of the search is either transparent to the inquirer or is briefly mentioned by citation only. Such management permits the funding of the resource to be carefully controlled by the host department. If the inquirer does not know the resource is available, he/she cannot request it specifically. In this way the researcher or librarian can determine the best resource to use in answering the question. The advantage of this method is that system usage can be expanded or contracted to conform to the amount of funding available; the disadvantage is that many information needs may go unserved if the inquirer does not know that a tool exists that will meet his/her needs. Unfortunately this disadvantage—underutilization—is a problem that perennially haunts libraries. Underutilization can be alleviated by an effective public relations or advertising campaign, and the Information Bank can be of great help in this area.

Another management concern which directly relates to cost consideration is: Should a subscription to the Information Bank be entered into independently, or is a consortium of users a better approach? Consortia do offer some savings, and such an option should be carefully considered prior to signing a contract. One of the major cost benefits of consortium participation is to be attained in the area of system access charges. Insofar as the monthly minimum use requirement is concerned, this requirement can be distributed among the members of the consortium. For example, with a minimum monthly use requirement of four hours of system use, there is a minimum charge of $200 per month for all individual subscribers. If there are ten members in a consortium, they would divide this $200, for a monthly minimum payment of $20 each.

In addition, Information Bank access rates go down with larger volumes of system use during a calendar month. Because individual use by members will be cumulative for the consortium as a whole, the lower rates associated with higher volumes of system use can be applied to each consortium member, for whom these low rates normally would be unattainable. The way in which monthly charges will be figured is as follows:

$$\frac{\text{Connect-time of individual member}}{\text{Total connect-time of consortium}} \quad X \quad \text{total to consortium}$$

Consortium participation will have no effect on the price of terminal and communication equipment except as may be arranged by the members of the consortium among themselves.

There is no doubt then that a consortium is a way to save money. It is also a very simple way to proceed, once the consortium signs the contract; any member may elect to begin Information Bank service at any time with no additional paperwork. It is not necessary for each member to sign an agreement form. We do ask that the Information Bank be notified that an additional terminal will be joining the consortium.

Each participating organization is assigned a separate password and identification code number for access to the Information Bank system. Thus, the proper code number can be entered for each individual search (this applies not only when using the system in person, but also for telephone requests to the "host" operator). In this way, monthly time charges are correctly allocated among group members. Each member's use is "metered" by his code number, and the organization is billed directly only for the time used.

If desired, the Information Bank can set up code numbers with subscribers according to departments or individuals within a member organization so that the subscriber can achieve even tighter control over internal cost allocations for Information Bank usage. Regarding equipment-rental and communications charges, the Information Bank will set up a billing system that best suits the group needs. Monthly billing can be direct to the "host" organization or divided in equal portions among group members.

For administration purposes, the Information Bank asks that the participants of the consortium select, designate or create a central administrative facility that will handle this billing function. This center will also be responsible for coordination of all Information Bank training, distribution of Information Bank printed materials, and for scheduling and participation in Information Bank activities such as subscriber workshops.

Presently, there are three operating consortia: the Foundation Librarians group in New York; Project Times in Norfolk, Virginia; and the University of California. The first two groups are sharing one terminal each: members from the Foundation Librarians visit the host terminal and run their own searches, while the Virginia consortium members call in their requests. The University of California intends to install terminals at a number of their campuses; in this way, several campuses may each incur savings by operating under a University of California umbrella contract. Consortium subscriptions are now under active consideration by the Pittsburgh Regional Library Council, the Michigan Library Consortium, the New England Library Board, and the Westchester Library System. If a library or information center director is considering Information Bank service, some thought should be given to either utilizing an existing consortium or creating one for this purpose.

Important management concerns have been mentioned throughout this discussion, such as system promotion, placement of hardware, charging for service, and concern for demand on the microform collection. I could also elaborate on a number of others: concern for any additional staffing time that may be required, preparation of the staff for automation, measuring and controlling staff reaction to the resource, monitoring system response and effectiveness for cost justification, etc. I have attempted to touch upon those thoughts and concerns that seem to be raised most frequently by our subscribers; I cannot begin to cover all the management decisions that must be made when planning for a computerized information system.

Similarly, there remain many day-to-day decisions and cost considerations that will arise as a subscriber organization becomes more and more familiar with the resource. Knowing the concerns of those presently engaged in operating on-line information systems, however, often helps a prospective user to plan better for this expansion. I have attempted to present the Information Bank not from the marketing point of view—which would tell you what the bank is, how you use it, when you can use it, its many applications within an organization—but from the user's point of view: How should I deal with this new resource? How are others handling it? I hope that by introducing you to the Information Bank's subscribers, much has been shown about the Information Bank itself.

REFERENCES

1. Greengrass, Alan. "Information Center Profile; The New York Times Information Bank," *Information* 6:29-30, Jan. 1974.
2. Funk, Charles. Personal communication, April 10, 1975.
3. Lipow, Anne. Personal communication, March 17, 1975.
4. Garvin, Andrew P. Personal communication, April 1, 1975.

Additional References

Longgood, William. "The New York Times; Terminals Come to the News-room," *Think* Aug. 1973, p. 22+.

Moghdam, Dineh. "The New York Times Information Bank in an Academic Environment and a Computer-Assisted Tutorial for its Non-Specialist Users." Ph.D. thesis submitted to the Graduate School of Library and Information Sciences, University of Pittsburgh, 1974.

Rothman, John. "The Times Information Bank on Campus," *Educom* 8:14-19, Fall 1973.

DONALD T. HAWKINS
and
B. A. STEVENS
Libraries and Information Systems Center
Bell Telephone Laboratories
Murray Hill, New Jersey
and
A. R. Pierce
Newman Library
Virginia Polytechnic Institute and State University
Blacksburg, Virginia

Computer-Aided Information Retrieval In A Large Industrial Library

This paper describes some of the experiences we have had with computer-aided information retrieval during the past years in the Bell Telephone Laboratories library network. In order to put the environment in which we work and the methods we use into perspective, a brief overview of Bell Laboratories and its library network will be given. Following this, some of our methods of information retrieval will be discussed in detail, including machine-readable output and computer-aided literature searching (both batch and on-line). After a short description of our indexing and dissemination methods, we will offer some suggestions on machine searching and draw some general conclusions.

Bell Laboratories is the research and development unit of the Bell System. It fulfills its responsibility for providing new communications systems and services and business information systems by carrying out research and development and systems engineering. The corporation is jointly owned by the American Telephone and Telegraph Company, which is the parent company, and the Western Electric Company, which is the Bell System's manufacturing organization. Bell Laboratories' annual budget is more than $600 million. It employs more than 16,500 persons stationed at eighteen locations. Many are located at Western Electric manufacturing facilities, where Bell Laboratories works closely with Western Electric in the final development and production of communications equipment.

Of the 16,500 Bell Laboratories employees, more than 7,000 are graduate scientists and engineers. A large number (approximately 2,000) of staff members hold the Ph.D. degree. The technical interests of the staff are very broad, including chemistry, physics, materials science, mathematics, computer and information sciences, psychology, electronics and electrical engineering, speech and acoustics, education and, of course, telecommunications. The company can therefore be viewed as a large and diversified community with a wide spectrum of information needs.

To help meet these information needs, a library network extending to all locations has evolved. The network holdings comprise approximately 150,000 book volumes and over 3,000 journal titles, 2,100 of which are current subscriptions. The network concept is emphasized in all library systems and services. For example, the resources of the twenty-eight units in the network are available to all. Those resources are visible in a printed book catalog which lists the holdings of all libraries in the network. Operating in a network mode means that services can be provided either locally or from a central point to all locations, depending on which method best suits a given situation. Most of the services provided by the library network are the traditional ones familiar to those engaged in library work. This paper will focus mainly on one of these services—the literature search—with a few preliminary words about reference service. (We are primarily concerned here with the outside literature, and not patents, engineering specifications, or other internal documents.)

Reference Service

The reference service is provided by reference librarians at those locations where the demand is heaviest. It is a local service, and as such is close to the user. It is well equipped to provide rapid answers to questions such as: Can you recommend a not-too-technical book on lasers? Which authors have cited my papers in the last two years? What is the current average wholesale price per pound of grey iron castings? Can you provide me with a detailed description of how a sphygmomanometer works? When a question is encountered which requires lengthy searching or specialized technical knowledge, it is passed to the literature searching service.

Literature Searching Service

The literature searching service is staffed by information scientists who compile bibliographies derived from the published scientific, engineering and business literature. The information scientists all have doctoral degrees in a technical field. Searches are undertaken in any area of need. The literature searching service is centralized at one location, and an attempt is made to have as many pertinent abstract journals as possible available there. An example of the diversity of search requests is shown by the titles of the following recent searches performed: aluminum joining, multidimensional scaling, mechanical properties of gold, infrared testing of integrated circuits, light scattering from fluids, minicomputer software, radiation effects on polymers. Figure 1 shows the subject distribution of ninety-three searches conpleted in an eight-month period.

Search Methods

This brings us to a description of the methods used by the information scientists in answering search requests. The possibilities are: (1) searching published abstracts and indexes manually; (2) using commercial searching services in the batch mode, receiving results in hard copy or machine-readable output; and (3) searching commercial data bases through an on-line terminal. Until 1972, traditional manual methods were used almost exclusively. Since then, however, a basic change has taken place, and machine methods have grown rapidly and now are the most often used. Hawkins's survey of the data bases used by the information scientists which covered the period from January 1972 to May 1973 found that machine retrieval methods were used in about one-third of the searches;[1] the figure is now well over one-half and is growing.

Machine Searching

Machine searching is the subject of an increasing number of publications. We will summarize what appear to be its major advantages and disadvantages. The advantages are:

1. Machine searching is exhaustive, but not exhausting. A machine can "see" all instances of a term in a data base. It can rapidly scan a large volume of information, and it does not get tired.
2. Normally, computers operate rapidly. We say "normally" because (on-line) system response can be degraded if a large number of users are trying simultaneously to gain access to the same data base or system, or if one user is tying up major resources. One must also be aware of

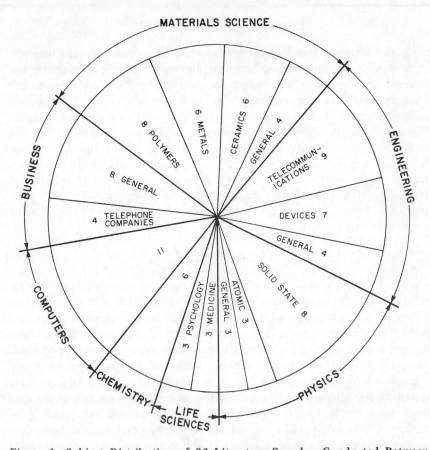

Figure 1. Subject Distribution of 93 Literature Searches Conducted Between April and November, 1973. (Figures indicate numbers of searches.)

system malfunctions, restarts, etc., which make the machine unavailable for periods of time varying from minutes to days.

3. The output is legible and well formatted, so that normally we do not have to expend clerical effort to edit or repackage it; the information can be given directly to the user. We frequently satisfy information requests with a list of references printed at the terminal and given directly to the requester.

4. There is the possibility of obtaining machine-readable output for further processing.

One disadvantage of machine searching may be the purchasing of services from outside suppliers. However, these disadvantages are minor annoyances accompanying a very advantageous facility. The negative aspects of obtaining machine searches from outside suppliers arise from the immaturity of the industry: suppliers are volatile. They tend to set their rates low in the hope of attracting a high volume of business, and then abandon the business when the volume does not meet their expectations. After deciding that a supplier offers a good service, investing time to study the system, and possibly writing interface programs to make the output compatible with your system, you may find after some months that the tape format has changed, or discover that the supplier cannot be depended on to make deliveries, or that they have simply shut up shop, and the investment made in adapting to the offering is wasted.

Assuming that a supplier is viable, we can list some of the other disadvantages of machine searching.

1. Not all important data sources are available. This disadvantage is being alleviated by the rapid growth in the number of computer-readable files being offered to users.

2. The data cover a limited time span. Very few files have information preceding the late 1960s: the government reports (National Technical Information Service) and American Petroleum Institute's files are notable exceptions. It might be expected that some data base producers would extend their files back in time, which would greatly aid retrospective searching. However, the clerical effort needed merely to keep files current is enormous and, with rising labor costs, it would appear that there is very little likelihood of such a backward extension. Cuadra observes from the standpoint of a search vendor that older data may not generate enough usage to justify economically keeping it on-line.[2] Some on-line systems drop off older data as new data are received, keeping only a fixed amount on-line. This may be useful for a market information file, or for a file listing new developments in a fast-moving technical area, but it severely limits its usefulness for retrospective searching.

3. The relevance ratio is sensitive to the search strategy, particularly in a batch system where one is unable to review the results as the search proceeds. Computers can generate a large volume of paper in a very short time, and one must use care in defining a search strategy which makes the output meet the requester's needs.

4. Finally, costs can be high, especially when many items are retrieved and one must pay a per-item charge. However, the costs of machine searching are often much lower than the costs involved in manual searching. Normally, therefore, cost is not a negative factor. Elman has recently studied this point, using the DIALOG system, and comes to the conclusion that the cost of the "average" manual search (if such a thing

exists) is $250, compared with $47 for the same search done by machine.[3]

We should point out that machine searching is not a cure-all. It cannot be used in every case. For instance, where a broad term exists in the thesaurus without a desired modifying or qualifying term, it will be necessary to use the manual approach in which the abstracts or printed index are scanned, rather than just titles. One recent example we encountered was in the preparation of a large bibliography on water,[4] where it was found impossible to separate by machine methods references on water of hydration, natural waters, etc., from those dealing with water as a pure substance or chemical entity.

One of the more hotly debated subjects in the area of machine searching is the question of the need for an intermediary, such as an information scientist, between the original requester and the computer terminal.[5] Our experience has been that such a person is needed to keep up with software changes, new data bases which become available, and changes in existing data bases. Efficient use of the system requires that the searcher know how to search the data, what elements in it are searchable, what output formats are available, etc. He or she must know which data bases allow free text searching, and which use a controlled vocabulary or thesaurus. A scientist or engineer will not normally use a system often enough to develop or maintain the skills necessary to exploit it efficiently. We have found that many original requesters are interested in machine searching, especially on-line searching, and that it is often useful, but not necessary, for them to be present when the search is performed. However, few of them wish to become burdened with details such as those we have just mentioned. We have observed that, as with any new method, users are at first enthusiastic, interested, and even fascinated, but when the learning of details becomes necessary or problems arise, the enthusiasm soon wanes and the user is quite glad to have the information scientist do the job.

We now turn to a description of some of the methods used in our information retrieval activities, focusing on computer-aided methods. Computer methods traditionally are divided between batch and on-line methods. In our own environment, we further characterize batch methods according to whether machine-readable output is obtained. After a general description of machine-readable output, we will discuss each type of searching in detail.

Machine-Readable Output

Increasingly, we find it appropriate to get the output of a search in machine-readable form (e.g., on magnetic tape) as well as, or instead of, in hard copy. One might ask why we desire machine-readable output. The answer lies in the desire to amortize the high cost of preparing a large bibliography by making the information it contains available to more than one user. Because of the breadth of Bell Laboratories' interests, there is usually a sizable potential audience for the bibliographies we produce. Quite often, a search request which is narrow in scope can be broadened to produce a bibliography of interest to a large number of people. Having search results in machine-readable form enables us to repackage the information into a uniform style, perhaps to add information from other sources, and then to provide an index to it using our permuted indexing system, BELDEX.[6] We also have a few ongoing bibliographies which appear at regular intervals, covering broad subjects of great interest to Bell Laboratories, e.g., optics and circuit theory. Because of their size, preparation of these bibliographies depends heavily on machine methods.

Some of the advantages and disadvantages of using the machine-readable output from a literature search should be identified. The advantages include:

1. It avoids redundant keypunching of data and the possible introduction of errors. Data once entered into machine-readable form do not have to be entered a second time, which avoids duplication of effort.
2. Large volumes of data can be easily manipulated by machine, as we have already discussed.
3. The cost of producing a bibliography is greatly lowered. Apart from the information scientist's salary, the greatest cost of bibliography production is data entry, such as keypunching. Using or modifying existing machine-readable data significantly reduces input costs.

The general disadvantages of machine searching listed above apply to machine-readable output as well. Some other disadvantages peculiar to machine-readable output are:

1. There are problems associated with magnetic tapes. The transfer of information from one computer installation to another is fraught with difficulties. Nothing is standardized—neither tape writing densities, record formats, character sets, nor terminology.

    The supplier must state the characteristics of the tape. Sometimes incorrect information is given, or words are used in a sense that is different from one's understanding of them. One must then ask a computer specialist to read the tape on the local machine. At the worst, he may be unable to do so if, for example, he does not have a tape drive for the appropriate density. Once the tape is mounted on a suitable drive, further traps await. Labeling, logical and physical records, record format (fixed or variable length, or spanned) and character set all must be properly characterized and handled by a local computer program. Moreover, a tape from an outside installation is likely to require little-used options in local utility programs. These are most likely to contain software errors. Finally, the tape may be physically defective: there may be spots on it where the magnetic coating is defective, or where the tape has been stretched.

If difficulties arise, the local expert may not be able to determine which of the various factors is responsible. Several weeks of interaction between you, the supplier, and the local computer center may be needed to clarify this.

2.   Once the tape has been successfully read by the computer, the data must be manipulated by a program to the desired form. You may find that the layout chosen by the supplier for the information fields is difficult to manipulate by your programs. For example, the author field may not distinguish between first names and family names, or between personal names and affiliations. Suppliers are also apt to change their formats or computers, both of which may be troublesome. If the format of the data has changed since the last running of the conversion program, the program will not run and must be altered, causing more delays. Sometimes the changes are not announced by the supplier, so that a debugging process must first occur. Errors in the data often occur and must be corrected.

3.   Still another disadvantage of machine-readable output is the one inherent in the loss of control over any process which depends on an outside supplier. If the supplier is having trouble with his tapes, his service bureau, or the data base producer, search results can be considerably delayed.

In spite of the disadvantages associated with using machine-readable output, we have found the practice to be most useful. We reiterate our opinion that the advantages far outweigh the disadvantages, especially after the initial difficulties have been surmounted and the process is on a production basis.

Interactive Retrieval

We now turn to a discussion of some of our experiences with interactive information retrieval. Our experience has been limited to the retrieval systems of Lockheed Corporation's DIALOG and System Development Corporation's ORBIT. We are relative newcomers to the ORBIT system, so that the following discussion mainly concerns the DIALOG system's behavior under our probing of its files. Our particular interest in the DIALOG system is based

Average Values

	Per Session	Per Search
Duration	21.2 min.	44.6 min.
Cost	$21.10	$44.50

Table 1. DIALOG Search Statistics, March-December 1974
438 Sessions, 208 Searches, 2.1 Sessions/Search

largely on its coverage of electronics, physics and computer literature through the INSPEC (*Science Abstracts*) data base.

We will now explore in detail some of the characteristics of our search experience. Table 1 gives a thumbnail sketch of the time and money spent during a ten-month period on the DIALOG system. We recorded 438 interactions with DIALOG on 208 search topics for 2.1 sessions per search. This is because many searches require data from more than one data base, and also because after reviewing the results one frequently gets a new idea and finds it profitable to return and try a new tack. These sessions averaged about twenty-one minutes, so that a search itself averaged forty-five minutes. This figure is in exact agreement with Elman's results. Further, after costs for TYMSHARE, batch print-out, and connect time are computed, we find that the rule of thumb "a dollar a minute" is a remarkably accurate gauge of how much one is going to spend on a search.

Of course, "average" figures may not be "typical." Figure 2 is a histogram of session durations for the 438 sessions included in this sample, and shows that the most frequent duration interval is somewhere between five and ten minutes and that, overall, 60 percent of the sessions took less than twenty minutes. It is those few very long searches that boost the average to twenty-one minutes. Total cost (see Figure 3) looks quite similar to the session duration histogram. Again, a few expensive searches—or a few generating voluminous output—boost the average cost.

We now turn our attention to what we were looking for in these 438 sessions. Figure 4 shows how the sessions were divided with respect to search objectives. The term *objectives* seems appropriate here because many of the sessions were concerned with objectives other than the traditional one of finding what has been written on a given topic. Notice, for instance, that slightly more than 15 percent of the 438 sessions were devoted to bibliometric research, and to demonstrations of the search system to members of the library staff. We feel that these in-house demonstrations are valuable in alerting our colleagues to the kinds of things that can be done easily using computer-aided searching. Often the knowledge that the facility is there and is

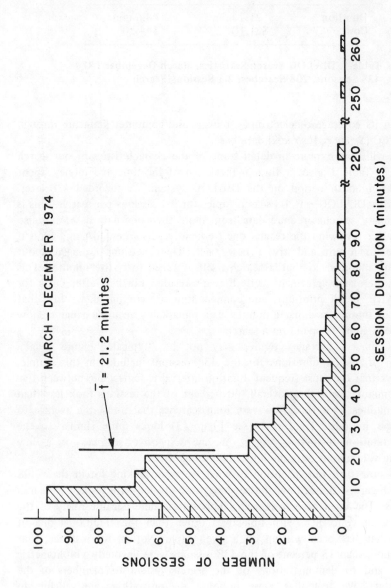

Figure 2. Session Duration Using the DIALOG System—438 Sessions

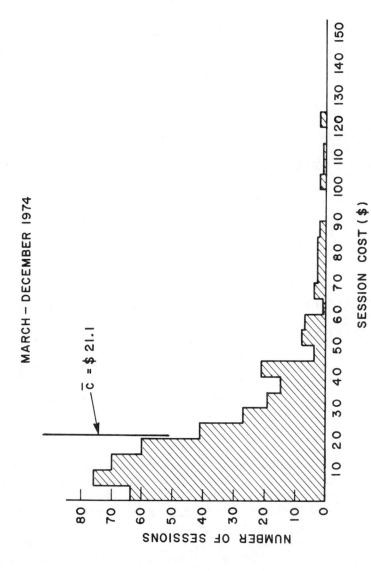

Figure 3. Session Cost Using the DIALOG System—438 Sessions

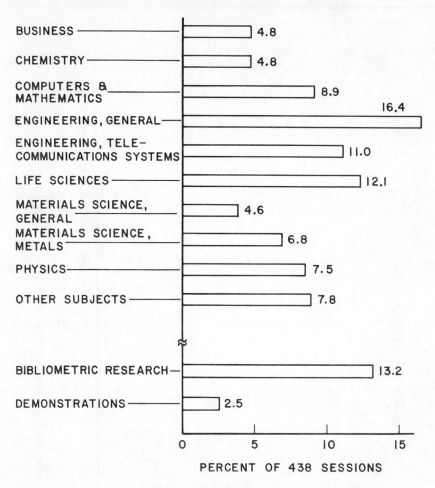

Figure 4. Search Objectives

relatively painless to use will prompt requests that might otherwise be done manually, or not at all. Using an interactive search system as an aid to bibliometric research also makes sense. Consider the following problem: we want to know how heavily various institutions publish in specific areas of science and technology. Using interactive retrieval, it is fairly straightforward to determine how many articles authored by institutions A, B and C, and appearing in core journals X, Y, and Z, were indexed by *Physics Abstracts*. Assuming that what is indexed by *Physics Abstracts* is, at least, an unbiased cross-section of current physics literature, it is then possible to gauge the relative publication activities of institutions A, B and C. Of course, in practice,

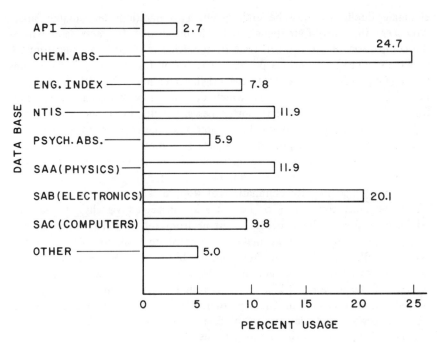

Figure 6. Data Base Usage (438 Sessions).

ing returns is reached; that is: When should a search be terminated? We have already noted that it is often profitable to search more than one data base, but we also know that searching too many data bases results in at best only a few additional references and, more often, considerable additional labor.

When machine search methods are being used, the problem becomes more difficult because of the volume of data that a search may yield. With manual searching of printed sources, items are acquired one at a time and filed; thus it is immediately known if an item is a duplicate. However, a machine search might yield hundreds of items at one time. An example from our recent experience will make the problem clear. Our search topic was from the field of materials science: "soft modes of lattice vibrations in solids." The first choice of data base was *Science Abstracts A*; a search yielded 200 references. A second choice was CA CONDENSATES, which yielded 100 references. By visual comparison of the items, it was found that 34 of the 100 items from CA CONDENSATES had not been retrieved from *Science Abstracts*.

This illustrates the nature of the problem; if the information scientist does not search the second data base, 15 percent of the potential material will be missed. If the second data base is searched, a laborious comparison to eliminate duplicates must be undertaken. Two questions immediately arise: Why were the thirty-four items not found in *Science Abstracts*? and Why is the comparison of the two sets (one from *Science Abstracts* and one from CA CONDENSATES) a laborious process? The reason for failure to retrieve items is complex; some causes are: (1) the original creation of the data base was at fault; (2) the item is of a type which does not receive exhaustive coverage from the data base supplier (reports, theses, patents, etc.); and, (3) retrieval failed because the item did not have appropriate descriptors. In the last case, inspection of the two output sets may suggest improvements in search strategy but, again, delay and expense are incurred if a new search is undertaken and a further hunt for duplicates must be made.

To understand why elimination of duplicates is expensive in time and effort, we must consider how the items are inspected visually. As they are originally acquired, the two sets of items from the two data bases are not arranged in a sequence that makes an immediate scan possible. Instead, a subsidiary file must be made from one or both, arranged by data elements that are considered least redundant. In practice, this might be the page number of the document. If a match is found on this element, a comparison is made on another one, probably journal title, and finally on volume number. Creating this inverted file for a set of several hundred documents is not cheap, whether machine or human methods are used.

The problems of information retrieval are compounded by the many different kinds of approximation any one data base makes to represent the documents it seeks to announce to potential users. If one tries to search *Chemical Abstracts* on-line he is not searching anything that looks like *Chemical Abstracts* at all. *Chemical Abstracts* on-line is the CA CONDENSATES file, which has far fewer entry points than the *Chemical Abstracts* volume indexes.

The CASIA (Chemical Abstracts Subject Index Alerts) data base does list all *Chemical Abstract* index entry points. However, CASIA has no abstract information. Figure 7 compares the two forms for the same document as they appear in CA CONDENSATES and the printed *Chemical Abstracts*. To further compound difficulties, different search systems usually treat any given data base differently. Although two competing data bases may have many journals and other sources in common, there is the problem that each will represent a given entry differently. Thus a strategy that worked well in one data base may prove to be fruitless when applied to another. On the other hand, the same strategy applied against multiple data bases (if this is possible) may be insurance that less is missed. Because of such hazards, interactive searching is very attractive since one can change logic or data bases as the search progresses, based on results accrued to that point. It is this feature—the ability to learn from mistakes and then take corrective action before the search logic freezes—that makes interactive searching so powerful and attractive a tool.

134257z **Improving the color of Ziegler olefin polymers**. Ainsworth, Oliver C., Jr.; Lochary, Joseph F.; Stain, Shelton D., Jr. (Dow Chemical Co.) **U.S. 3,773,743** (Cl. 260–94.9F; C 08*f*), 20 Nov 1973, Appl. 796,153, 03 Feb 1969; 5 pp. Olefin polymers contg. ≤500 ppm metallic catalyst residues which characteristically discolor on exposure to high temps. were stabilized against discoloration and degrdn. during and after high temp. processing by intimately contacting the polymer with about 0.5–1.5 wt. % (on polymer) OH compd. contg. 0–12 C atoms and ~50–2500 ppm $C_{≤2}$ Lewis base boiling ≥100°, and processing the polymer contg. the alc. and base at a temp. above the polymer softening point to improve its color. Thus, *polyethylene* **[9002–88–4]** prepd. by low pressure polymn. in hexane in the presence of a 1:1 *titanium trichloride* **[7705–07–9]**≏ *–triisobutylaluminum* **[100–99–2]** catalyst was steam distd. to remove the hexane and a substantial portion of the catalyst, and the polymer contg. 30–50% water was dried to <0.1% moisture to give samples contg. 76 ppm Ti residues, and having Milner color 72.6. Each sample was charged to a feed section of an extruder operating at 190–250°, and as the sample passed into the extruder from the feed section, a mixt. of water and an org. base contacted the polymer. Thus, 200 ppm *calcium stearate* **[1592–23–0]** and 1.4 wt. % water were added to polymer in the feed section, and extruded to give a product with Milner color 86.5. When the Ca compd. was increased to 2000 ppm, the color was 89.6.

```
CA08024134257Z
   Improving the color of Ziegler olefin polymers
   AUTHOR: Ainsworth,  Oliver  C.,  Jr.,  Lochary,  Joseph  F.,  Stain,
Shelton D., Jr.
   SECTION: CA036006    PUBL.-CLASS: P    COVERAGE: 1
   JOURNAL: U.S.    CODEN: USXXAM    PUBL: 731120    PAGES: 5 pp.
   DESCRIPTORS: Lewis  base  stabilization  polyolefin,  color  stability
polyolefin,  degrdn resistance polyolefin,  polyethylene color stability
   PATENT-NO: 3773743    APPLIC-NO: 796,153    DATE: 690203    CLASS:
260-94.9F, C 08f
   ASSIGNEE: Dow Chemical Co.
```

Figure 7. Chemical Abstracts and CA CONDENSATES Representation of the Same Abstract. (Reproduced by permission of Chemical Abstracts Service.)

Batch Searching

We use batch searching when the data we require is not available to us through interactive search techniques. For example, not being members of the American Petroleum Institute (API), we search this data base by going directly to API with our problem, and let them do the probing. In one way, not having access to a rarely used file (in our case, the API files are rarely used) is something of a benefit. It is unlikely that we would ever be as effective information intermediaries as the specialist on that file for what is, to us, an exotic file. This example can be generalized to libraries or information centers not having subject specialists on staff. In this case the batch information centers offer the advantage of the review of profiles by specialists.[7]

BATCH RETRIEVAL WITH MACHINE-READABLE OUTPUT

As mentioned before, obtaining search results in machine-readable form results in great economies in the preparation of our bibliographies. Beyond saving the direct costs of keypunching, recall the additional considerations favoring this approach: (1) errors are not introduced through the transcription process, and (2) no one should have to keyboard material that someone else has already keyboarded. The first point is self-evident, and the second focuses on what Weiner called the "human use of human beings."[8]

Figure 8 shows in some detail the steps involved in utilizing machine-readable output. First, the results are received on magnetic tape from one or more sources and converted to a format compatible with BELDEX, our KWIC (Key Word In Context) indexing system, using a FORTRAN program. Next, a BELDEX run is made and the results are reviewed by the information scientist. (More details on BELDEX operations are discussed below.) Typically, a copy of the preliminary BELDEX results is forwarded to the original requester at this point, giving him something with which to get started. Now the information scientist has an opportunity to review the results, delete the irrelevant entries and perhaps to classify the bibliography into sections. Additional data—possibly from either another batch search or manual searching—can be integrated with the original results. For this purpose we utilize a very powerful on-line tool called QED (Quick EDitor).[9]

QED is a string-oriented, interactive programming language. For example, it is easy to find and correct spelling variants using QED. Consider the Americanization of the word *colour*. We require the program to find each occurrence of *colour* and substitute *color* for it. The code to achieve this looks strange but is brief: 1,$s/colour/color/. It is read: "On every line of the file containing the string 'colour,' substitute the string 'color' and now all lines have been Americanized." Such fixes were used in a recent bibliography on color television, for example.

Because QED is a programming language, we can run stored QED programs against new input data that are in nonstandard formats and convert the data to our standard BELDEX form algorithmically.

The interactive feature of QED means that we always know the current status of the file we are working on. Gaps in time between editing and running the edit program do not exist; thus, we are not required to dredge up from a hazy memory a recollection of what was going on. Interactive editing lets us focus our attention on the job at hand. For example, consider the chore of adding subject class codes to items in a bibliography. Frequently, this is done after the information scientist has reviewed the preliminary BELDEX output. This would be a difficult task using punched cards since each card would have to be found and removed, the subject code punched, and the card refiled. Using QED, the editor works through the file using a stored program

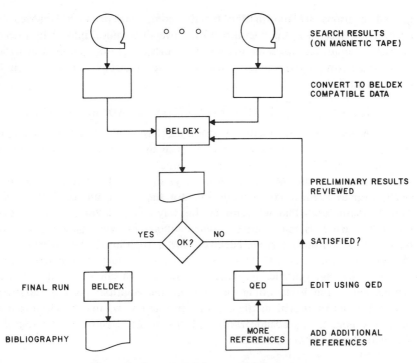

SEARCH RESULTS
(ON MAGNETIC TAPE)

CONVERT TO BELDEX
COMPATIBLE DATA

PRELIMINARY RESULTS
REVIEWED

SATISFIED?

EDIT USING QED

ADD ADDITIONAL
REFERENCES

Figure 8. Steps in Bibliography Production.

that requires only enough keystrokes to specify the subject code of a particular item. Occasionally the data the program sees are anomalous, and then
it pauses in midstream. For batch processing this would be a disaster and the
job would abort, but in time-sharing there is the opportunity to back up, fix
the unexpected data string, and continue to a successful conclusion. The
process of review and correction continues until the information scientist is
satisfied that the product is of acceptable quality.

We also make considerable use of tapes purchased from commercial
sources—in particular, the INSPEC (Information Service in Physics, Electro-
technology and Control) tapes. Here we are doing much less ambitious
searching than Lockheed, System Development Corporation, the Illinois
Institute of Technology Research Institute, and the Knowledge Availability
Systems Center offer. Information systems developed at Bell Laboratories for
this purpose select all entries from a data base by the journal in which the
article appeared. This journal/subject filter scheme is a major part of the input
for our largest current awareness bulletin, *Current Technical Papers*. This
bulletin appears twice each month in five sections. On the average, the total
number of papers announced in all sections exceeds 2,000 per issue. These

filtered citations are reformatted by the computer and then reviewed by information specialists for relevance to the overall technical information needs of Bell Laboratories. We seldom allow our roles as information intermediaries to be taken over by machines: their job is to collect references, ours is to judge them.

BATCH RETRIEVAL WITH NO MACHINE-READABLE OUTPUT

Our usage of this mode of searching has declined rapidly as on-line systems have grown. We do not foresee much use of it in the future, either. The reason for this concerns volume of output: (1) if the output is great, it will be costly to process further (i.e., keypunch), and (2) if the output is small, we may spend a considerable sum for the search, but get little return. This does not mean that we consider this way of operation to be a bad one, but rather that it is not adapted to our methods. Indeed, a batch search with only printed output is quite adequate for a traditional SDI (selective dissemination of information) service, or for libraries which do not have access to a time-sharing computer terminal or system. Such libraries or information centers are spared what would be for them the additional cost of cumputer terminal rental or purchase. High quality profile review, and the fact that one needs no more than pen and paper, explain why this type of batch retrieval is the right choice for many searches.

Dissemination

We now address the question of what to do with a mass of references collected on a given topic in response to a search request. This is not a trivial matter: in many cases we accumulate 1,000 to 2,000 references for a given search.

When the data collection phase is complete, the resulting references may be an unorganized mass, derived perhaps from different sources, with duplicates, inconsistent styles of citation, typographical errors, etc. Some may be recorded on computer printout, some may exist in machine-readable form and some will be on hand-written records. It is useless to distribute this confused mess. Our task is to organize it, index it, and provide easily readable copy in a form that lends itself to reproduction. Our product will then not only serve the original requester optimally, but will also be available to others who might find it useful.

The task is composed of two operations: (1) mechanical—get the words onto the page; and (2) editorial—correct errors and provide an index. As previously noted, we have at our disposal a computer aid, BELDEX, developed specifically for these purposes. It creates good copy with numerous indexes to facilitate editing and utilization as a bibliography.

The input to BELDEX is a machine-readable file of records, each tagged to show its nature, e.g., title, author, or bibliographic citation. Furthermore, the group of records constituting one item of the bibliography must be together, with the last one marked to show that it is the last. BELDEX, when presented with a file of such records, performs the following tasks:

1. Report generation—the creation of the bibliography itself, a complete listing of all the references. The user has great freedom in specifying format.
2. Indexing—BELDEX can create indexes for any data elements. The most important is a permuted title index (KWIC); another very important one is an author index. These two usually form part of the completed bibliography; other optional indexes, such as a source-journal index, are sometimes used as editorial aids.

In many cases, we wish to list the bibliography items in some order other than the order of acquisition or input. Possible choices are by a subject breakdown, by author, or chronologically. BELDEX will create this order by sorting the input material using tags that are present on the items.

However, we feel that one of the more important accesses to the information in the bibliography is the permuted title index (KWIC). We have devoted much effort to developing BELDEX indexing into a powerful tool with the well-known advantages of KWIC while avoiding some of the disadvantages. For example, BELDEX provides a stop-list of nonentry words, such as *a, the,* and *of*; all KWIC programs have such a list. However, in BELDEX, the list is generalized to an "action" list. The most common action is indeed "stop"—do not use the word to create an index entry—but the user also has other options, such as: "go"—create an entry only if the word is on the list; create *see also* references; replace unauthorized terms with authorized ones; or ignore prefixes for indexing purposes. These are some of the built-in options. For special needs, others may be implemented within the framework of the action list.

KWIC indexes are useful for error correction because a typographical error will often be displayed in the index in the context of correct words from other entries. Figure 9 shows how this can be used to detect spelling errors, or inconsistent volume/year information in a citation.

BELDEX was created by the Libraries and Information Systems Center at Bell Laboratories; our center maintains it and uses it daily. Consequently, it is continually evolving. As new needs are perceived, they are incorporated into the system. Over a fifteen-year period, this system has become a flexible, powerful and reliable tool.

```
LIGHTNING ARRESTERS OF LIGHT WEIGHT CONSTRUCTION.
COAXIAL CABLES STRUCK BY  LIGHTENING.
COAXIAL CABLES STRUCK BY  LIGHTENING.
HOTOELECTRIC DETECTOR OF  LIGHTING.
STERS WITH SWITCHING AND  LIGHTING OVERVOLTAGES UNDER NE
UDY OF THE PARAMETERS OF  LIGHTNING.
VOLTAGE STATIONS AGAINST  LIGHTNING.
                          LIGHTNING AND SURGE PROTECTION
                          LIGHTNING ARRESTER CURRENTS.
TCHES AND PERFORMANCE OF  LIGHTNING ARRESTERS.        SWIT
E DESIGN OF HIGH VOLTAGE  LIGHTNING ARRESTERS.
CS OF 8.4-KV, VALVE-TYPE  LIGHTNING ARRESTERS AGAINST ST
        REPRESENTATION OF  LIGHTNING ARRESTERS IN MODEL T
                          LIGHTNING ARRESTERS OF LIGHT W
                          LIGHTNING PERFORMANCE OF OVERH
        THE PROTECTION FROM  LIGHTNING STRIKES OF COMMUNICA
        THE PROTECTION FROM  LIGHTNING STRIKES OF COMMUNICA
NSMISSION SYSTEMS DUE TO  LIGHTNING STROKE ON OVERHEAD G
KV LINES AGAINST DIRECT  LIGHTNING STROKES.
                    HOW  LIGHTNING-SAFE ARE YOUR BURIED
ON DISCONNECTING A LONG  LINE.              CLASSICAL
RGE ANALYSIS OF OVERHEAD  LINE CABLE SYSTEM WITH SKIN EF
OF OVERHEAD TRANSMISSION  LINES.
        SHIELDING 400 KV  LINES AGAINST DIRECT LIGHTNING
LTAGE ON DISCONNECTING A  LONG LINE.              CLAS
```

Figure 9a. Permuted Title Index Showing Typographical Errors.

```
003   ELEC ENG 49(4): 33-4 (APR 1972)            SHIE
005   ELEC ENG JAP 90(4): (JUL-AUG 1971)         SWIT
015   ELEC ENG JAP 91(4): 201-8 (JUL-AUG 1971)   SPAR
001   ELEC ENG JAP 91(4): 69-78 (JUL-AUG 1971)   DIGI
004   ELEC INDIA 11(6): 31-5 (JUN 1971)          TREN
008   ELEC LIGHT POWER 49(8): 42-4 (MAY 1971)    HOW
002   ELEC REV 191(1): 16 (JUL 7, 1972)          PIPE
006   ELEC TECHNOL 4: (1970)                     CLAS
013   ELECT COMMUN 40(3): 381-4 (1965)           ESTI
023   ELECT COMMUN 40(3): 381-4 (1965)           ESTI
022   ELECT ENGNG JAPAN 84(7): 47-56 (JUL 1964)  SURG
026   ELECT ENGNG JAPAN 86(2): 39-46 (FEB 1966)  SURG
025   ELECT ENGNG JAPAN 86(7): 62-71 (JUL 1966)  SURG
018   ELECT ENGR 39(5): 37-43 (AUG 10, 1962)     LIGH
020   ELECT TIMES VOL 137: 409-10 (MAR 17); VOL  SURG
010   ELECTR WORLD 179(9): 42-5 (MAY 1, 1973)    SURG
024   ELEKT STANTSII (12): 85-6 (DEC 1966) (IN R EXPE
012   ELEKTR STANTSII (11): 67-9 (NOV 1973) (IN  AN O
014   ELEKTRICHESTUO (4): 80-3 (1969) (IN RUSSIA THE
028   ELEKTRICHESTUO (4): 80-3 (1969) (IN RUSSIA THE
009   ELEKTRICHESTVO (1): 28-35 (JAN 1964) (IN R LIGH
011   ELEKTRICHESTVO (3): 67-70 (MAR 1973) (IN R THE
019   ELEKTRIE 14(5): 163-5 (MAY 1960) (IN GERMA REPR
017   ELEKTRIE 17(1): 21-4 (JAN 1963) (IN GERMAN MEAS
027   ELEKTRIE 23(10): 431-3 (OCT 1969) (IN GERM TEST
```

Figure 9b. Journal Citation Errors and Inconsistencies.

Need for Standards

We now turn to a discussion of those areas of machine searching that need improvement. One possible solution to the problem of differences in data bases and suppliers is uniform standards. Standards allow the searcher to plan searches intelligently. They remove the haphazard approach of finding response "slow," data cells "down" (so that full bibliographic data cannot be printed), or files not updated because the supplier has not "gotten around to it yet." A more fundamental standard would be to announce that the goal for a system is to be up and available, say, 99.5 percent during scheduled hours.

More rigid standards are also needed in the data bases themselves. Figure 10 is a dictionary display from CA CONDENSATES using the DIALOG system. We are expanding around the term *cross*. Note that terms E1, E2, E36, E40-E43, E45, and E9-E12 are misspellings of proper variants of *cross-link*. It is reasonable that such errors happen, but is it reasonable that they remain uncorrected? The problem is one of divided responsibility—there is little motivation for the search vendors to fix up someone else's files. If Chemical Abstracts Service were to correct the data base, the corrected version would have to be reloaded by the search vendors at considerable cost. These spelling mistakes are potentially serious, since most on-line searching systems are based solely on string matching techniques. We would also make a plea for standards for treatment of authors' initials, uniform abbreviations for periodicals, etc. The number of variations in these from one data base to another is astonishing.

The Information Utility

The 1974 conference of the American Society for Information Science had as its theme "Information Utilities." This approach views bibliographic data base publishers and search system vendors as being part of a chain which in many respects resembles a public utility. It is therefore reasonable to state that these organizations should be accountable to their users. It should also be noted that many data base publishers enjoy pre-eminences in certain technical areas. It is unlikely that any group could challenge Chemical Abstracts Service or INSPEC and produce a competitive product. Indeed, such duplication would be wasteful and almost certainly counterproductive. It is better to have one excellent source of chemical bibliography than two good sources. Because of this pre-eminence, however, there should be strong mechanisms to ensure the maintenance of high and compatible standards throughout the information industry. Search vendors should be persuaded to establish, publish, and follow standards which minimize the user's problems and ensure maximum compatibility, service to service and data base to data base.

Ref	Index-term	Type	Items	RT
→ E1	CROSLINKED		1	0
−→ E2	CROSLINKING		1	0
E3	CROSS		4613	0
E4	CROSSARM		1	0
E35	CROSSINGS		12	0
−−→ E36	CROSSINKING		1	0
E37	CROSSITE		3	0
E38	CROSSLAID...................		1	0
E39	CROSSLAND		1	0
−−→ E40	CROSSLIINK		1	0
−→ E41	CROSSLIINKING...............		2	0
−→ E42	CROSSLINBING		1	0
−→ E43	CROSSLING...................		1	0
E44	CROSSLINK...................		263	0
−→ E45	CROSSLINKAABLE		1	0
E46	CROSSLINKABILITY		2	0
E47	CROSSLINKABLE		119	0
E48	CROSSLINKAGE		33	0
E49	CROSSLINKAGES		8	0
E50	CROSSLINKED		1049	0
E51	CROSSLINKER		271	0
E6	CROSSLINKERS		8	0
E7	CROSSLINKING		3956	0
E8	CROSSLINKINGS		4	0
−→ E9	CROSSLINKINNG		1	0
−→ E10	CROSSLINKKING		1	0
−→ E11	CROSSLINKLING		1	0
−→ E12	CROSSLINKNG		1	0
E13	CROSSLINKS.................		97	0
E14	CROSSMIXING		1	0
E15	CROSSOPTERYGIAN		1	0
E16	CROSSOVER		54	0
E17	CROSSOVERS		4	~

Figure 10. DIALOG EXPAND Listing Showing Misspellings in CA CONDEN-SATES Data Base

We can now draw some general conclusions. Certainly, the computer has had a major impact on the business of information retrieval, and it has made its mark at Bell Laboratories. Machine searching has made many advances in the past two years. If used judiciously and with full awareness of the pitfalls it offers many advantages. It saves time and money, it is comprehensive, and it can be fast.

However, machine searching is not necessarily the best method in all cases. Many searches still have to be done manually, such as those going back in time beyond the scope of the available data bases, and those not well defined, requiring browsing of a data base or index. (The eye can skim a page much faster than a 30cps terminal can print. Serial presentation can never surpass the random retrieval of the eye.)

On-line systems generally give better results than batch systems. They offer the searcher the ability to learn from intermediate results as the search proceeds. They also offer the opportunity to combine terms—in a Boolean sense—in ways which are impossible using printed indexes. However, machine searching systems suffer from errors and inconsistencies in the data bases, as well as from a lack of standards. As vendors become more aware of these shortcomings, we are confident that improvements will occur, and we look forward to an increased exploitation of what is already an indispensable tool of a literature searching service.

REFERENCES

1. Hawkins, Donald T. "Bibliographic Data Base Usage in a Large Technical Community," *Journal of the American Society for Information Science* 25:105-08, March-April 1974.

2. Cuadra, Carlos A. "SDC Experiences with Large Data Bases," *Journal of Chemical Information and Computer Sciences* 15:48-51, Feb. 1975.

3. Elman, Stanley A. "Cost Comparison of Manual and On-Line Computerized Literature Searching," *Special Libraries* 66:12-18, Jan. 1975.

4. Hawkins, Donald T. "A Bibliography on the Physical and Chemical Properties of Water, 1969-1974," *Journal of Solution Chemistry* 4:623-743, Aug. 1975.

5. Barber, A. Stephanie, *et al.* "On-line Information Retrieval as a Scientist's Tool," *Information Storage and Retrieval* 9:429-40, Aug. 1973.

6. Lowry, W. Kenneth. "Use of Computers in Information Systems," *Science* 175:841-46, Feb. 25, 1972.

7. Schipma, Peter B. "Searching Costs [letter]," *Special Libraries* 65:6A, Aug. 1974.

8. Weiner, Norbert. *The Human Use of Human Beings; Cybernetics and Society.* Rev. ed. Garden City, N. Y., Doubleday, 1954.

9. Deutsch, L. Peter, and Lampson, Butler W. "An On-line Editor," *Communications of the ACM* 10:793-99, Dec. 1967.

R. BRUCE BRIGGS
Manager of Programming and Operations
Campus Computing Network
University of California
Los Angeles

The User Interface
For Bibliographic Search Services

The user interface for a bibliographic search service includes the entire set of user-service interactions, from initial phrasing of the information needs to final review of the results. This interaction has occurred in reference libraries for many years, and an investigation of the literature in this area yields a wealth of information. Analysis of this information, however, shows that while the functions of the reference process are fairly well defined, the process itself is not, and is essentially left to the judgment of the reference librarian.

When analysis is limited to literature on computer-based bibliographic search services, a similar picture emerges. This literature deals primarily with technical and operational problems, as might be expected, because these were the initial problems facing the designers and developers of this comparatively new service. Attention was given to the user interface, but not with the same studied approach that was given to other components of the system. Nevertheless, as solutions to the technical and operational problems are being found, the importance of understanding the user interface is being increasingly appreciated. The desire to serve the user better, the attention given to automating components of the user interface, and the growing interest in information networks of libraries and bibliographic search services are just some of the reasons for attaining this understanding.

In December 1973, the University of Georgia (UGA) and UCLA began a joint research project with funding from the National Science Foundation to study the user interface for computer-based bibliographic search services. There were two objectives of the study: (1) to study the existing user interfaces and to model the search services at UGA and UCLA after them, and (2) to propose one or more models for the user interface for a multi-disciplinary bibliographic information network. The study teams at each institution were composed of staff who had participated in the design and development of the respective bibliographic search centers.

The search center at UGA is known as the Georgia Information Dissemination Center (GIDC). It serves twenty-five institutions of higher education in the University System of Georgia, as well as numerous governmental agencies, other academic institutions, and commercial organizations throughout the United States and in several other countries. The search center at UCLA is known as the Center for Information Services (CIS), and serves twenty-two institutions of higher education in the University of California and California State Universities and Colleges system, as well as numerous private colleges and universities, governmental agencies, and commercial organizations throughout the United States. The GIDC operation is the larger of the two, offering current awareness searches on eleven data bases and retrospective searches on sixteen data bases; CIS presently offers only current awareness searches on five data bases.

Both centers provide trained reference librarians or information specialists to assist the user in obtaining service from the search center. GIDC has four information specialists on its staff who handle search queries primarily for the University of Georgia, Georgia State University, commercial users, and the smaller two- and four-year institutions in Georgia. These four staff members have graduate degrees in the subject matter areas appropriate to their data base specializations; none has had previous library work experience. Search profiles for users at the Georgia Institute of Technology and the Medical College of Georgia, as well as for users at remote sites in Ohio and New York, are prepared by reference librarians at those locations who have received workshop training on computer-based retrieval from the GIDC staff. CIS has two staff members whose primary responsibilities are to train reference librarians in the various institutions served, and to advise the reference librarians how to handle difficult or unusual search requests. These two staff members occasionally work directly with users who do not other-wise have access to a trained specialist; however, the vast majority of users work through the forty-five reference librarians in the institutions that CIS serves.

RESEARCH STUDY METHODOLOGY

The approach used for this research study was for the teams at each institution to operate independently, but in parallel. The purpose was to achieve a certain degree of redundance, to create a check-and-balance function, and to provide a means for determining intercenter differences. The two teams maintained a close interaction by meeting regularly during the period of the study.

The study was divided into three phases: data collection, analysis, and model development. The data collection phase was designed to collect information on all aspects of the user interface, with an emphasis on the interaction process between the user and the reference librarian or information specialist (hereafter called the intermediary). All data collection instruments used were developed for purposes of this study; some were developed jointly and used by both teams (to provide a basis for intercenter comparisons), while others were developed and used by one of the two teams. All instruments were field-tested prior to the beginning of the data collection period. The jointly developed data collection instruments were:

User Information Form This form was completed by users prior to the user-intermediary interview, and included information such as: a prose formulation of the user's question; suggested keywords, synonyms, and excluded terms; search type requested (current awareness or retrospective); and information about the user (e.g., previous experience with computer-based search systems, occupation, intended use of results, etc.).

Post-Interview Questionnaire for Intermediaries This form was completed by the intermediary immediately following an interview with a user. Its purpose was to gather information on the intermediary's perception of different aspects of the interview, such as the user's information needs, the nature of the user's question, the user's attitude, the expected performance of the profile, and the general nature of the interview.

Follow-Up Questionnaire for Users This form was sent to each user involved in the study following receipt of at least one set of search results from each data base specified for the user's profile. The questionnaire was intended to obtain the user's general reactions to the search service, to the usefulness of the results, and to the elapsed time from the interview to receipt of results. Users were also asked to make additional comments and suggestions.

Both teams also tape-recorded user-intermediary interviews and transcribed them for subsequent analysis. Users' permission was obtained beforehand, and each was assured that the tapes would be used solely for research purposes.

The analysis phase began about two-thirds of the way through the data collection period with a preliminary analysis of data collected at that time to test procedures. The analysis was, in part, data-directed, and had the objectives of describing in detail the components of the user interface, and of providing the basis for development of the models. The particular analysis techniques used were independently selected by the two study teams and then compared for completeness and consistency.

It was not known at the outset whether the analysis would lead to the specification of one or more than one model of the existing user interface. Conceivably, there could be a different model for each center's interface, or even a different model for each intermediary. In any event, after modeling the existing user interface, the objective was then to propose one or more models for the user interface for an information network.

RESULTS

The complete results of this study are presently being compiled for the final report to the National Science Foundation and were not available at the time this paper was written. Therefore, the results presented in this paper, unless explicitly stated otherwise, are based on the UCLA study team's findings. These results are grouped into six major categories: user characteristics, intermediary characteristics, interview process, users' questions, profile coding, and search results.

User Characteristics

The user population is predominantly academic with 44 percent of the users being graduate students, 37 percent academic researchers, and 33 percent faculty members. (The categories overlap in some cases because users were asked to check all applicable titles.) The nonacademic segment is primarily staff (17 percent of all users), which consists of administrators and technical and general support staff.

Results regarding the purpose of the search also reflect the predominantly academic character of UCLA's users: 74 percent of the profile searches were performed for research projects, 36 percent for master's degree theses, 27 percent for teaching purposes, 27 percent for bibliographies for publications, and 32 percent for personal bibliographies. Less popular uses of the search results were seminars (10 percent), class projects (11 percent), term papers (8 percent), doctoral dissertations (7 percent), and patent searches (2 percent). Eighty-eight percent of the users were new to this particular retrieval system. Most of them (95 percent) had heard of computer-based retrieval, but 56 percent indicated no previous experience with it and only about one-tenth (11 percent) were highly experienced.

The users' attitudes and expectations were relatively good: most (71 percent) exhibited an interested (optimistic) attitude toward computer-based retrieval; the majority (88 percent) expected the service to be of some value, but not perfect. Most (85 percent) of the users did not change their attitude during the interview.

The most significant difference reflected by the data collected was the user's estimated ability to write his own profile. While 79 percent of the users believed they could write their own profiles, the intermediaries thought only 48 percent of the users could do so, and the researchers thought only 36 percent could do so. However, more than one-half of the users who believed they could write their own profiles qualified it by saying this was true if they had help from the intermediary. Fifty-four percent of the users indicated they would want to write their own profiles. It is interesting to note the lack of any significant correlation between users estimating that they could write their own profiles and wanting to write their own profiles. Seventy-seven percent of the users responding said they could write their own profiles (on their own, with an analyst, or with a good manual), but 33 percent said that although they could do it, they did not want to.

Intermediary Characteristics

Of the thirty-eight intermediaries who responded to this questionnaire, 81 percent have graduate degrees in library science and 74 percent are currently working as reference librarians. All seven of the intermediaries who do not have library science degrees do have graduate degrees in other fields and/or experience with library systems and data processing.

The intermediaries' profile writing experience, including experience with other computerized information retrieval systems, ranged from less than three months to more than two years. More than one-half of the intermediaries have been writing profiles for over one year, with 34 percent having more than two years of experience. From a list of five alternatives (apprenticeship, workshops or seminars, self-taught, manuals, and other), the intermediaries were asked to check all applicable means by which they were trained for writing profiles. The responses indicated that the two most frequent means were through workshops or seminars (76 percent) and profile writing manuals (71 percent). Sixty-three percent said they were self-taught and 29 percent received training through an apprenticeship. Fifteen percent listed other means of training, e.g., library school courses.

The intermediaries identified five major problem areas which specifically related to their roles as intermediaries between users and CIS:

1. *Users* Seven of the intermediaries listed problems getting the users to participate, specifically in expressing their needs in the initial interview, in providing additional information for inclusion in the profile, and in providing feedback concerning satisfaction with the citations retrieved.

2. *CIS* Seven intermediaries listed as a problem the delays and slow turn-

around time from the time the profile is submitted to CIS to the arrival of the first set of citations.

3. *Time* Ten intermediaries reported that the added time needed for user interviews, profile construction and coding, output review, and profile revisions presented a problem since they were also expected to continue to perform their regular professional duties as reference librarians. Mention was also made of the burden of the additional time which had to be devoted to "clerical" tasks such as recordkeeping, forwarding output to users, etc.

4. *Training* Seven intermediaries listed the need for more training by CIS staff in profile construction and profile refinement, with emphasis on the individual data bases. Intermediaries also felt that they needed more technical information on how the computerized information retrieval system works to better prepare them to answer the broad range of questions asked by the users.

5. *Subject Knowledge* Although many intermediaries referred to the problem throughout the questionnaire, five intermediaries specifically mentioned that the main problem they encountered was that the required depth and breadth of the subject knowledge to write successful profiles was much greater than that needed to be a "successful" reference librarian.

In light of the problems listed by the intermediaries, it was surprising that a significant controversy appeared in their responses to questions which sought their opinions on automating parts of the user interview and profile construction process. There was a 50-50 split (15 percent did not answer this question) between the intermediaries who thought parts of it could and should be automated and those who felt (some rather strongly) that no part of the process should be automated. None of the intermediaries felt that the entire interview could or should be automated; however, many suggested supplementary on-line capabilities, i.e., thesauri, sample data bases and syntax checking, which could be used during the interview and profile construction and coding process.

The Interview Process

EVENT ANALYSIS

Transcripts from eight interviews tape-recorded for test purposes were reviewed to produce a list of significant events that occur in the user-inter-

Event Number	Event	Number of Occurences
25	INFORMATION REQUEST CLARIFIED BY USER	259
24	ANALYST REQUESTS CLARIFICATION OF INFORMATION NEEDS	236
38	SEARCH STRATEGY DISCUSSED	232
55 U	USER REQUESTS TUTORIAL	160
28	SEARCH TERM SELECTED BY USER (PROMPTED)	143
18 A	DISCUSS SUBJECT AREA TERMINOLOGY AND RETRIEVAL CAPABILITY	126
27	SEARCH TERM SELECTED BY USER (VOLUNTEERED)	79
59	INDEXING POLICY OF DATA BASE DESCRIBED	100
67	OTHER	99
18 B	USER TUTORIAL ON SUBJECT	90
37	VOCABULARY (PROFILE CODING AIDS) CONSULTED	80
17	REFER TO USER INFORMATION FORM (OTHER THAN REQUEST STATEMENT)	78
6	SEARCH PROCEDURE DESCRIBED	77
5 A	SEARCH SYSTEM DESCRIBED	62
29	SEARCH TERM SELECTED BY ANALYST (USER AGREEMENT)	52
26	SEARCH TERM SELECTED FROM REQUEST FORM	37

Figure 1. Most Frequent Events

mediary interview. This analysis produced a list of seventy-two "expected" events. Then, with appropriate checks to minimize inconsistencies due to subjective judgments by the study team, each transcript was analyzed and the identified events were recorded in the margin in their chronological sequence. These event sequences were then analyzed to determine whether patterns within the sequences existed.

Computer programs were written to yield frequency listings of individual events, and of subsequences (see Figure 1). The analysis then proceeded to determine the relationships between events, e.g.: How often does event A precede event B, and how often does it follow event B? A surprising result of this analysis was that if event B had the highest frequency of following event A, and event C had the highest frequency of following event B, the frequency of the sequence A, B, C was not similarly high. This observation was consistent for all event sequences.

The study team then tried to produce a graph where the nodes were the events, and the arcs indicated the number of times (above a given threshold) that one event preceded or followed another. The result was dubbed the "spaghetti model" by the UCLA team (see Figure 2). Examining the matrix associated with this graph, the team found two salient characteristics: (1) the matrix is not sparse, and (2) most values are small. These characteristics are indicative of a nondeterministic process.

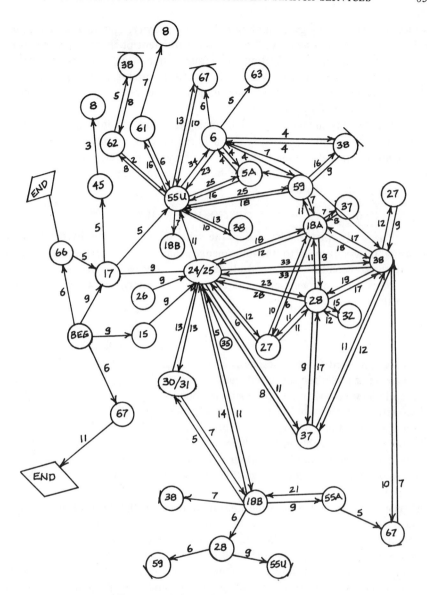

Figure 2. Graph of Event Sequences

Using a different approach, the team grouped events into categories which were descriptive of the functions of the events, resulting in the following categories: system description, data base selection, search type selection, clarification of request statement, request statement negotiation, profile construction, search strategy formulation, tutorial activity, diverting activity, and other (miscellaneous) activity. The five most frequent of these categories were profile construction, clarification of request statement, request statement negotiation, search strategy formulation, and tutorial activity. A graph of these categories shows profile construction to be central to the interview process (see Figure 3).

The conclusion drawn from this analysis is that the interaction between the user and the intermediary is not a linear process, despite descriptions to the contrary in the literature. The process is nondeterministic, and is characterized by the ability of the human intermediary to adapt it to the particular needs of the user.

VALUE OF THE INTERVIEW

The study attempted to assess the value of the interview by determining whether it was helpful to the intermediary and to the user, and by determining what conditions existed during the interview which influenced its helpfulness. The following elements correlated to interviews which were helpful to the intermediary:

	Kendall Coefficient
User was prepared for the interview	.77041
User expressed his literature needs well	.65731
User left interview with an optimistic attitude	.48618
User actively participated in the interview process	.47495
User understood and participated in profile construction	.43951
User was knowledgeable in his subject area literature	.42780
User had written a clear information request	.38563
User was important in term suggestion during the interview	.26558

Interestingly, the data shows that, although many of the users asked questions and provided information freely when discussing their subject area, clarifying their search requests, etc., they become less active and needed to be prompted more when the activity centered on profile construction. During the interview, other than during profile construction activity, 45 percent of the users were curious and willing to cooperate with the intermediary and asked some questions, but gave information mainly when prompted. Only 11 percent of the users seemed reluctant to ask questions and gave short answers to the intermediaries' questions. During the profile construction activity, only 15 percent of the users were interested in the details of profile construction, understood Boolean logic and citation term scanning, and were able to participate in the profile construction process at this level. Fifty percent of

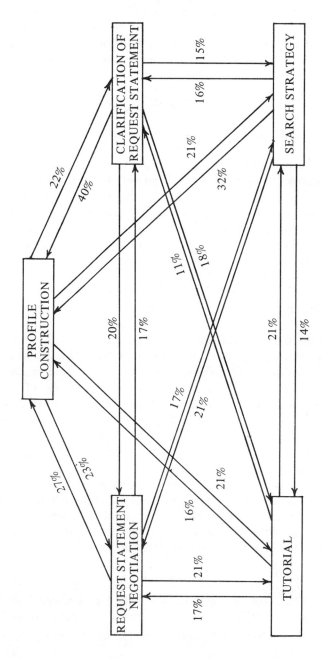

Figure 3. Interaction Between Major Event Categories

the users had a lesser understanding of profile retrieval mechanisms and, although they were able to discuss and participate on a less sophisticated level, they were able to provide the intermediary with suitable terms for inclusion in their profiles. Thirty-five percent of the users did not understand profile construction and were thus only minimally able to discuss and participate in the construction of their profiles.

The Users' Questionnaire

On the user information form, users were requested to prepare a prose statement of their question. In evaluating these statements, the intermediaries perceived no discernible weaknesses in 49 percent of the cases, while the researchers perceived no weaknesses in 41 percent. The perceived weaknesses in the remaining cases were predominantly that the statements were either too broad (18 percent) or too narrow (27 percent). In very few cases did the user either not know what he wanted (8 percent), or expect too much of the retrieval service (6 percent). The researchers judged that 81 percent of the written statements of interests were clear, but that only 40 percent of them were complete enough for profile preparation.

The scope of users' questions as observed by the intermediaries and researchers was split into broad (37 percent and 42 percent respectively), average (33 percent and 29 percent, respectively) and narrow (28 percent and 29 percent, respectively). When forced to choose, users preferred a broad search (89 percent) for high recall to a narrow search (11 percent) emphasizing precision. Both the intermediaries (76 percent) and the researchers (69 percent) confirm this in their perception of user preferences. (The user's stated preference and the intermediary's observation of it correlate with a coefficient of .31 and significance of .001; researchers' perceptions correlate with users' with a coefficient of .38, significance .001.)

Although UCLA is not presently offering a retrospective search service, 17 percent of the users specified that they wanted only this type of service; 25 percent specified that they wanted only current awareness service; and 58 percent specified both. Intermediaries and researchers tended to categorize most users (79 percent and 59 percent, respectively) as wanting either a moderate number of references (50-100) or a large number (greater than 100) and did not view users' expections as being substantially different.

Profile Coding

Nearly two-thirds (63 percent) of the profiles were coded completely after the interview, and 27 percent of the profiles were coded partially during the interview and completed after the interview. Therefore, a total of 90 percent of the profiles were coded partly or entirely after the interview. Typically, then, when the intermediaries begin to code a profile, they have received input from the user in writing via the user information form and in person via the interview. The intermediaries indicated they may also consult other resources for help in coding the profile.

The study team attempted to ascertain the extent to which all the identified potential inputs to the profile are included in the profile. They began by looking at the coded profile and by diagramming its structure. Then, they became familiar with the user information form and the interview transcript, and described the profile's correlation to both these forms of user input.

The profile and the user information form are:

Rating	Percentage
very similar	15
generally similar	31
slightly similar	23
dissimilar	29
unable to determine because of technical nature of subject	0
not reported	2

The profile correlates to:

Rating	Percentage
the user information form almost exclusively	4
the user information form more than the interview	13
both about equally	27
the interview more than the statement of interest	36
the interview almost exclusively	2
neither very much	17

Thus, in the study team's judgment, the profile is generally similar to the user information form less than one-half (46 percent) of the time, and only slightly similar or dissimilar in about one-half (52 percent) of the cases studied. Also, while 76 percent of the profiles are derived from both the user information form and the interview, the interview is more important in a larger number of cases (38 percent as compared to 17 percent). Sixty-five percent of the profiles were described as having been derived strictly (13 percent) or largely (52 percent) from user-supplied information. Twenty-seven percent were derived largely from the intermediary's ideas but generally confirmed by the user in the interview. Eight percent were based primarily on the intermediary's concepts and apparently not confirmed by the user. Regarding term selection, the user contributes either primarily (50 percent) or in cooperation with the intermediary (40 percent) in 90 percent of the profiles; the intermediary contributes either primarily (10 percent) or with the user (40 percent) in 50 percent of the profiles.

Besides the intermediary and the user, what other inputs to the profile coding process are there? Word counts show that 32 percent of a profile's subject terms are not specifically mentioned either in the interview transcript or on the user information form. These search terms may be derived from the intermediary's previous knowledge of the subject, from various printed resources, or from conversations with other persons. The data concerning these sources of input to the profile are somewhat scattered, but can be summarized as follows:

1. For 51 percent of the profiles, the intermediaries describe their previous knowledge of the subject as generally familiar (41 percent) or very familiar (10 percent).
2. For 80 percent of the profiles, the intermediaries report using profile coding aids (thesauri, word frequency lists, coding manuals).
3. Texts or reference books were consulted by the intermediary while coding 36 percent of the profiles.
4. Dictionaries were consulted in order to code 37 percent of the profiles.
5. Personal contacts, besides the user, were resources employed in 13 percent of the profiles.
6. Other resources were consulted for 18 percent of the profiles.
7. During the interview, hard copies of the available data base(s) were consulted in 21 percent of the cases; other profiling aids were used during 28 percent of the interviews.

It is also relevant to note that the percentage of profile words from sources other than the user information form and the interview apparently does not affect the profile success, i.e., there is no statistical correlation.

There is a large degree of variation in the time spent by the intermediary in constructing the profile. The mean is about 1½ hours, but the median is just a little over one hour. The range is from ten minutes to seven hours, with 75 percent of the profiles taking between one-half hour and two hours.

The 44 profiles studied in detail search the following data bases: Current Index to Journals in Education (38 percent), Research in Education (38 percent), Social Science Citation Index (38 percent), Biological Abstracts (67 percent), BioResearch Index (58 percent), Chemical Abstracts—organic chemistry sections (38 percent), Chemical Abstracts—inorganic chemistry sections (15 percent), and CAIN—agricultural citations (4 percent).

Sixty-nine percent of the profiles search tapes produced by different suppliers. However, only 48 percent are constructed to search differently on one or more data bases; 23 percent use different primary retrieval mechanisms; 13 percent use different subject vocabularies.

The primary retrieval mechanisms used in the coded profiles are: subject words in citation titles and indexing phrases (98 percent), subject codes (44 percent), authors (60 percent), referenced citations (21 percent), journal titles or abbreviations (15 percent), and subject words in citation abstracts (6 percent). The profiles include the following refinements (some are not possible on certain data bases): language restrictions (23 percent), journal names–included (13 percent), journal names–excluded (4 percent), and publication type–patent, book, articles, etc. (2 percent).

After the profiles were coded, the intermediaries expected that 40 percent of them would yield approximately the number of references the user wanted, 31 percent would yield more, and 25 percent would yield less. They also expected that 46 percent would need revisions for improved precision, 28 percent would need improved recall, 22 percent would need no revisions, and 1 percent would need to be completely rewritten.

Search Results

The information obtained on search results will be presented in three sections: user reaction, intermediary reaction, and feedback and revisions.

USER REACTION

The overall reaction of the users to their search results was fairly positive in many respects:

1. Ninety-one percent of the users described their search result as either very useful (37 percent) or of some use (54 percent).
2. Eighty-one percent reported that references were retrieved which were not previously known.
3. Fifty-six percent indicated that they considered the retrieval system a fast means of performing the search; 69 percent indicated that the search had saved them time.
4. Although 39 percent of the users received fewer relevant citations than expected, 64 percent reported the number of citations was about right to be manageable and useful.
5. Eighty-nine percent of the users ranked convenience among the three most important of the things they liked. Thoroughness and the printed compilation of references were also ranked important by more than one-half the users.

Significant negative reactions by the users included the following:

1. About one-half (48 percent) of the users described the elapsed time from construction of the profile to receipt of the answers as too slow, but only one user said it was not useful due to slowness. Thirty-three ranked slowness among their top three dislikes.

2. A total of 31 percent of the users were dissatisfied with the number of citations; 19 percent said they received too few and 12 percent reported too many.

3. Forty-four percent of the profiles could, in the users' opinions, benefit from the revisions; however, only 25 percent wanted revisions made soon; others said they did not have time, it was too late, or it was not worth the effort.

4. Twenty-five percent of the users were not sure if they will continue the search service; 8 percent said they do not expect to continue.

5. The most frequently ranked dislike was "no way to judge completeness." It was ranked among the top three important dislikes by 65 percent of the users (41 percent ranked it most important).

There are two indications that users are more severely discouraged by too few references than they are by too many. All of the users reporting too many answers still described the search as of some use. But 59 percent of the users reporting too few or no answers found their result of little or no use. Nearly all users reporting too many answers indicated that revisions were in order, but about one-half of the users with too few or no hits felt they did not have time to determine needed revisions, or it was not worth the effort, or it was too late to be of help to them. Understandably, users getting too many citations hold more hope for getting useful results from their profile than users receiving too few or no hits. The correlations between questions on the user follow-up survey reveal an interesting phenomenon: a user tends typically to be either generally pleased with the search results and system or generally disillusioned and critical.

INTERMEDIARY REACTION

Results from the first several searches are usually mailed to the intermediary for review purposes before being forwarded to the user. The intermediary reviews the output, notes problems and needed revisions, and then forwards the output to the user. Records kept by intermediaries participating in this study show that they spend an average of forty minutes in reviewing the output for each profile; thus, the intermediary usually has an idea of the usefulness of the search output independent of any feedback received from the user.

The intermediaries were fairly positive in their evaluation of the search results, although slightly less so than the users themselves. Twenty-one percent of the profiles were rated very successful by the intermediaries, 43 percent moderately successful, 19 percent marginally successful, and 4 percent unsuccessful. The intermediaries felt the success of 12 percent of the profiles was as yet undetermined when the questionnaire was collected.

Intermediaries indicated that 55 percent of the profiles usually retrieved references which were satisfactory both in number and relevance. They indicated that 14 percent retrieved many irrelevant references, 22 percent retrieved few relevant references, and 4 percent retrieved no references. It was interesting to observe that the intermediaries, like the users, react more unfavorably to too few hits than to too many. Fifty-three percent of the profiles receiving "few relevant hits" were described at best as only marginally successful, but 73 percent of the profiles receiving "many irrelevant hits" were described at worst as "moderately successful."

FEEDBACK AND REVISIONS

A considerable amount of activity after the first search results is well within the norm for CIS profiles. There is some indication that even more activity— e.g., output review, discussion with users, and profile revision—would result in more satisfied users. There is also indication that more participation by the users may be beneficial.

Intermediaries spent an average total of 41 minutes reviewing output for each profile; the range was 0 to 185 minutes. Note that the data are somewhat inexact, since intermediaries had received different quantities of search results at the time the data were collected. During the data collection period, 39 percent of the profiles were revised. For the revised profiles, an average of forty-eight minutes was spent by the intermediaries making from one to eight textual revisions per profile. The predominant number of revisions was one; however, the extent of the changes included in each revision submitted can vary greatly. Only 6 percent of the profiles were completely rewritten.

The need for revisions does not correlate with overall usefulness; 34 percent of the profiles studied were described as useful but with revisions still needed. However, there is a relationship between revisions needed and the number of answers received; when users described their searches as receiving approximately the right number of answers to be useful they tend not to require revisions as frequently as those receiving too many or too few. Thus, a significant number of users are finding their results useful, but are desiring revisions to bring the number of citations down or up to the desired level.

For most of the revised profiles, the user suggested changes or worked with the intermediary on the revisions. User participation was apparently a motivation for revisions. The researchers found postsearch activity by the user notably lacking, describing 44 percent of the profiles as "needs to be reviewed by the intermediary and user together." This apparent lack of communication regarding the search result is further evidenced by: (1) the reported lack of feedback from users to intermediaries (intermediaries cited lack of user feedback as affecting the success of 34 percent of the profiles; the researchers observed that only 33 percent of the users gave feedback to their intermediary); (2) for 39 percent of the profiles, the intermediaries reported that the need for revisions was undetermined at the time of the survey; (3) for 12 percent of the profiles, the intermediaries reported the profile success as undetermined; and (4) for 9 percent of the profiles, the intermediaries reported the quality and quantity of hits retrieved as unknown. The inability of the intermediary to assess the need for revisions and the lack of user feedback correlate quite strongly; about one-half of the profiles described as affected by the lack of user feedback could not be assessed by the intermediary in terms of needed revisions. Similarly, about one-half of the profiles for which the intermediary could not determine the need for revisions were affected by the lack of user feedback.

MODEL OF THE EXISTING USER INTERFACE

The model of the existing user interface was developed jointly by UGA and UCLA, and is based on the analysis of the data collected in the study. The model, as shown in Figure 4, can be considered to have two major components: the presearch activities, represented by the upper half of the figure; and the postsearch activities, represented by the lower half. Both of these components involve interactive processes and, based on the findings of the study, are shown as nondeterministic processes.

In the presearch activities, administrative procedures generally occur first, and profile entry and editing occur last. No predictive statements can be made about the order of the remaining activities, except to say that they are generally interspersed throughout the presearch activities. The study showed that both the informational activities and the data base and search type selection activities were largely supportive of other activities.

The study did not collect and analyze as much data on the postsearch activities as it did on the presearch activities; however, the data collected did indicate that this portion of the user interface was also nondeterministic. The supportive activities occur in this component also because of the tendency of users to add or drop data bases, to request a current awareness search after a retrospective one (or vice versa), and to require additional information as to the need for revisions.

This model describes the existing user interfaces at both UGA and UCLA, and may be descriptive of the interface at other search centers. The interpretation of the model will, of course, vary from center to center, and even from case to case within a center.

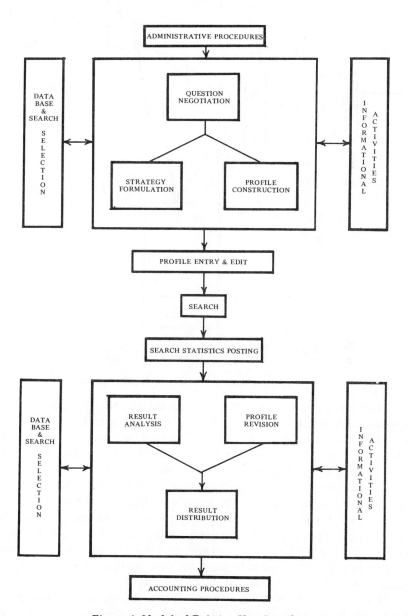

Figure 4. Model of Existing User Interface

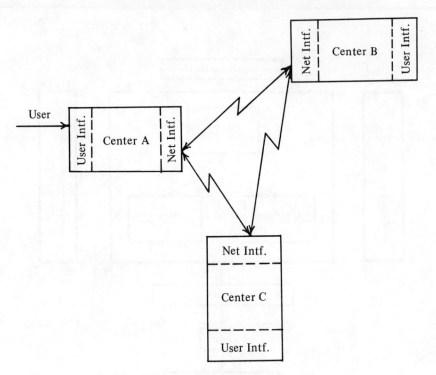

Figure 5. Proposed Network Configuration

User Interface for a Network Environment

The study teams considered a number of different network configurations before choosing to propose the one shown in Figure 5. In this configuration each center in the network maintains two interfaces, one for the user and one for the network. The purpose of this user interface is the same as for existing user interfaces—to transform the user's query into an effective profile, and to assist the user with result analysis and profile revisions. In fact, this interface can be similar to the center's existing one. The network interface provides a standard mechanism for communications among centers by transforming outgoing profiles and results into exchange formats, by transforming incoming profiles and results into the local formats, and by serving as a mechanism for remote users to reach the user interface. The structure of a search center in this environment is shown in Figure 6.

For example, a user may contact center A and request searches of several data bases, some of which are available at center A and the remainder of which are available at center B. The user's query is transformed into a profile in center A's format as a result of the user's interaction with center

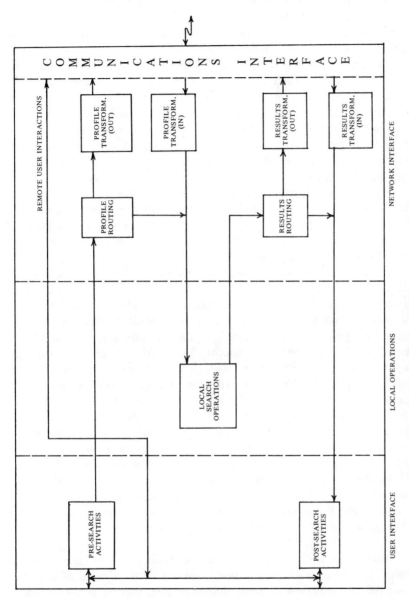

Figure 6. Search Center in Network Environment

A's user interface. This profile is then used to search against those data bases available at center A. Concurrently, the profile is transformed by center A's network interface to an exchange format and sent to center B for searching against the remaining data base specified. Upon receipt, center B's network interface transforms the profile into center B's local format and processes it. Results from center B are transformed to an exchange format and sent to center A where they are transformed to the local format for printing and delivery to the user. There are several advantages to this approach: users interact with only one interface—that of the center most convenient to them—but still have access to all of the services available in the network; centers can maintain their existing user interface; the configuration is modular, allowing for expansion or contraction of the network; and the configuration is adaptable—changes to one center's user interface do not necessitate changes throughout the network.

Components of the network identified by this study as requiring standardization prior to the realization of the network are: data base elements and content, the exchange language for profiles, the communications protocol for control parameters (e.g., data bases to be searched, search type, etc.), and the specifications for transmission of results.

One conclusion of this study is that the intermediary serves a necessary and vital role in the user interface. Some users do not, however, have trained intermediaries available to them. In addition, intermediaries indicate that sometimes they need assistance in areas such as profile construction, language features, and processing procedures. For these reasons, a system specialist is proposed for the network environment. The system specialist would have in-depth knowledge of the profile language, profiling aids and data bases, and would have general subject knowledge. Where appropriate, several system specialists with more specialized subject knowledge could be used. The function of the system specialist would be to serve as a consultant and resource person for both users and intermediaries, and to serve as the primary intermediary for users (e.g., remote users) not having access to an intermediary. The method of communication between the specialist and the user could be through interactive terminal messages, via telephone or, as is being experimented with by one existing center, via headphones to users at interactive terminals. The interaction between the user or the primary intermediary and the system specialist can be represented by Figure 7.

This study really only scratches the surface of the user interface problem. The study teams believe that there are a large number of areas that warrant further study, and an equal number of areas that are as yet unstudied. For example, the recorded interviews contain a wealth of information about the interactive process; only a small portion of this information was gleaned

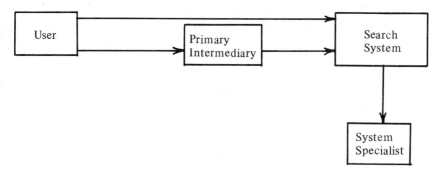

Figure 7. Role of System Specialist

for analysis. Also, the emphasis of this study was on the presearch activities, but the postsearch activities are equally important. Now that the technical and operational problems initially experienced by search centers are under control, attention needs to be turned to the human engineering aspects of the service.

DAVID M. WAX

Director

Northeast Academic Science Information Center

Wellesley, Massachusetts

NASIC And The Information Services Librarian: Room In The Middle

As activity related to the provision of information has increased and become more complex in recent decades, the role of the intermediary between the information producer and the information user has similarly become more complex and specialized. The referee, the journal editor, the abstracting and indexing service, the publisher, the bookstore owner and the librarian are all examples of educated intermediaries who have a significant impact on the quantity and kinds of information resources available to the user. This paper will consider the activities of two types of intermediaries in one of the newer and more complex information delivery processes: the computerized bibliographic search.

Initially, I shall discuss a new role for a traditional intermediary—the reference librarian. Later, I shall describe and evaluate an attempt to define an organizational intermediary, of which the Northeast Academic Science Information Center (NASIC) is a prototype, developed specifically in response to this new information service. While this discussion emphasizes the delivery of machine-readable services in the academic community, most of the comments are equally applicable to the special library and public library communities.

Perhaps the easiest way to introduce the role of these two participants is to locate their place on the search service continuum (see figure 1). It is important to bear in mind that information both begins and ends with the members of the research community, for it is they who produce the infor-

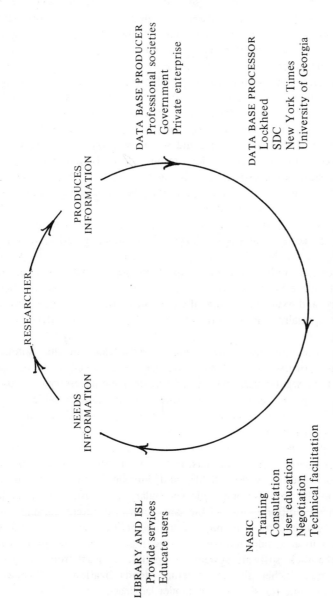

Figure 1. The Search Service Continuum

mation in the form of articles and reports, and they who need the search results in the form of citations and abstracts.

The activities of the data base producers and processors have been discussed in great detail in the literature on libraries and information science, so this discussion will relate to them only insofar as they create both the resources which make computer-based searching possible and the environment which makes the other intermediaries necessary.

In the past year there has been extensive interest expressed in the possibility of direct user access to the information resources available through on-line searching. Indeed, this represents a basic aim of the User Requirements Program of the National Science Foundation's (NSF) Office of Science Information Service. If we could somehow provide for direct "bench scientist" access to the information resources, it is thought, we could eliminate the staff costs associated with the need to have two people understand the problem and could obtain more effective search results based on the user's greater awareness of his own needs.

It is possible, of course, for the end user to learn the literature, the data bases, and the access system in sufficient detail to be an effective searcher. However, because of the substantial time required for training, this would be a costly process if applied to a large number of users. Furthermore, each user would have to make fairly intensive use of search services in order to maintain his knowledge and expertise, so that the amount of time spent conducting the search—and especially time spent connected to the computer—could be minimized.

In the academic environment, and in most cases in the commercial sector, the users of machine-readable search services are likely to be occasional users rather than regular users who could maintain the necessary expertise for efficient searching. One can conceive of only two situations in which it would be possible for these occasional users to conduct a search through direct personal interaction with the search system.

The first situation would require that the data base producers work together to standardize their products, not only in terms of searchable fields, uniformity of material within fields, and indexing philosophy, but most importantly in the area of compatible vocabulary. The difficulty of the latter can be seen in the differing uses of the same term in different disciplines—e.g., the use of the term *power* in physics and in political science. At the same time, this situation would require that the major data base processors or suppliers make their software systems compatible, at least from the perspective of the user, either through internal standardization or through the development of some translation or compiler language.

The second possibility for direct user access lies in the development of a compiler that would not only make the systems compatible, but would also relate the user's information needs to the appropriate data bases and translate the search question into appropriate strategies with appropriate vocabularies to search these data bases on whichever systems they happen to be accessible.

For reasons of professional pride, entrepreneurial competition, and lack of outside funding to underwrite standardization projects, neither of these situations is likely to occur within the foreseeable future; for reasons of vocabulary incompatibility, they may never occur. Fortunately, a reasonable alternative to these conditions presently exists in the form of the intermediary who is aware of the content of the data bases, the means by which the various systems can be employed for access to the data bases, and appropriate techniques for searching the specific data base on a particular software system.

THE LIBRARIAN AND THE LIBRARY AS INTERMEDIARY

For several years there has been an ongoing debate as to whether this knowledgeable intermediary should be a subject specialist (engineer, physicist, chemist) who has been trained in a particular access system, or a literature specialist (reference librarian) who has sufficient familiarity with the literature of several disciplines as well as training on one or more access systems. Most of the NASA- and NSF-funded search service centers have relied on subject specialists; but with the advent of on-line searching in hundreds of universities, government agencies, and commercial firms, reference and special librarians are now responsible for the great bulk of computerized bibliographic searching.

In most governmental and commerical libraries, the librarian as an on-line searcher represents only an extension of the traditional role of the special librarian. The conducting of personalized bibliographic searches has long been an activity of the special librarian; the on-line search is merely a new and less costly means of providing this service.

In the academic environment, however, with the single major exception of the biomedical library, the reference librarian has not traditionally performed personalized search services for either faculty or students because of the lack of staff time and resources for such services. As a result, the role of the on-line searcher is a totally new one for the academic reference librarian.

Not all of the librarians with whom NASIC has dealt have been particularly well suited to adapt to this new role of information services librarian (ISL). Some, for example, are afraid of the terminal; others are reluctant to type at the keyboard in the presence of a user. A few are unwilling or unable to undertake the intellectual effort associated with conceptualizing a search problem and creating an appropriate search strategy. On the whole, however, the academic librarian has adapted well to this new activity. Of the sample of sixty-four ISLs whom NASIC has trained to date, the staff considers more than 80 percent to be at least adequate in undertaking searches and more than 50 percent to be very good or excellent. While the members of this group are in many cases administratively or self-selected participants, this nonetheless represents significant documentation of the capability of the traditional reference librarian to fulfill this new role.

The introduction of machine-readable bibliographic searching into the academic library also creates a significant change for the library itself. Most of the NASIC-affiliated institutions (see Appendix) already report a noticeable increase in the use of the serials collections and a clear increase in interlibrary loan activity. Indeed, we have come across some libraries that have been unwilling to initiate computerized searching or to publicize or promote the services once implemented for fear that they will place an unmanageable burden on present staff, both because of the time required to provide the search services themselves and because of their impact on other library services.

The introduction of search services has also forced academic libraries to face the issue of charging for information services. Every NASIC participant is recovering at least part of the charges associated with the provision of search services. At one end of the spectrum, several libraries have provided sub-sidized—but never free—searching as a special introductory offer; at the other end, one library has been recovering overhead costs as well as out-of-pocket costs resulting from the provision of these services. Approximately 80 percent of the NASIC libraries, however, are now or always have been charging the user the out-of-pocket costs associated with searching, while allotting funds from the library budget to cover staff and equipment costs. Thus it appears that academic libraries have adopted the position that the staff capability of offering the service is an overhead item, no different from the staff capability of reference librarians or catalogers, but that the unique or personalized aspect of the service—the out-of-pocket costs—should be paid by the beneficiary of these custom services.

The initiation of computer-based reference services has also required the library to adopt a more active role in user education and service promotion. Because these services imply a new means by which the user obtains infor-mation and also require that he pay for the information services, the library is obligated to make the user aware of the existence of this new local capability and to demonstrate the value of the computerized search. Every NASIC library has been engaged in this type of service promotion, albeit with varying degrees of intensity, relying heavily on actual on-line demonstrations as an educational technique. The fact that this technique has had success in attracting users to on-line search services may lead to similar types of active educational and promotional efforts for other library services.

One should not conclude from this rather optimistic evaluation of the introduction of computerized bibliographic search services into some eighteen academic libraries in the Northeast that this type of personalized, pay-as-you-go service is a forerunner of a reorganization and reformulation of library functions in the academic setting. At this time, this new service constitutes a small addition to traditional library services, generally accounting for less than one percent of library expenditures. The MIT libraries, providing service at the rate of forty to fifty searches per month, constitute one of the more intensive academic users of on-line search services in the country.

A major reason for this low level of activity, of course, is cost. Where search services are heavily subsidized or free, as in the case of MEDLINE, there is much more intensive use of machine-readable searching. A second reason for limited use in the academic setting is the cutback in nonbiomedical research funds which could be used to pay for search costs. A third reason is the lack of awareness among potential users of the existence and value of computer-based bibliographic searching. Acquaintance and initial use of search services stimulate further use, a situation which is documented by the increasing dependence of the biomedical research community on MEDLINE and related services and by the high level of repeat use of NASIC services.

These and other issues underlie the justification and need for an organization such as NASIC to serve as an intermediary between the suppliers of computer-based search services and the academic libraries at which services are delivered to users. It is to the less obvious role of this second intermediary that we now turn our attention.

NASIC AS INTERMEDIARY

NASIC was conceived by the New England Board of Higher Education (NEBHE) and funded by NSF's Office of Science Information Service for the express purpose of increasing access in the academic community of the Northeast to computer-based bibliographic search services. NASIC is the last of the NSF-funded science information dissemination centers and the only one not to become involved with direct in-house processing of bibliographic tapes.

The intent of the original NASIC proposal was to make existing service capabilities accessible to institutions that would never become directly involved in tape processing themselves. This was to be accomplished by working through the university libraries and training reference librarians to become knowledgeable intermediaries between the users and the systems. A secondary aim was to make existing NSF- and NASA-funded processing centers economically stronger by directing to them the "business" generated in the NASIC-affiliated institutions. The first aim, that of making search services more accessible in the academic community of the Northeast, remains the primary goal of the program; the plan to direct the region's searching "business" to the off-line processing centers has been abandoned.

In the period between the conceptualization of the NASIC program in November 1971 and the post-funding organization of the program in July 1973, the on-line search services offered by Lockheed and System Development Corporation (SDC) became available to the general public. Analysis by the NASIC staff of the alternatives led to the conclusion that, for reasons of speed, cost to the user (particularly for multivolume retrospective searches) and, most importantly, improved search effectiveness resulting from interaction with the data base, on-line searching was the more valuable service for the academic library to offer to its users. Accordingly, the NASIC staff initiated discussions with university librarians and with representatives of the search service vendors to determine the appropriate role, if any, for an intermediary organization in assisting the academic library to offer more effective on-line search services. These discussions resulted in a range of NASIC activities, including training, administrative consultation, user education, negotiation and technical facilitation.

The training activity is of primary importance, since it is a prerequisite for the reference librarian to serve as an ISL. While both Lockheed and SDC do offer training sessions, their programs are directed more toward the special librarian than toward the academic reference librarian. The vendors assume that the librarian is familiar with the techniques of searching and with the organization and content of the relevant data bases. Therefore, they concentrate on system-related materials (logging on, search commands, output commands, system messages) and some discussions of data base peculiarities. Since approximately 90 percent of SDC and Lockheed searchers are special librarians in commercial or government agency libraries, this is a reasonable plan for a general training program.

However, this type of program does not meet the needs of the academic reference librarian who is to become an ISL. As previously indicated, it is unusual for academic librarians regularly to perform manual searches. Therefore, the conceptualization and organization of the search must be part of any training program oriented toward the academic library community. Also, with limited experience in searching, the academic librarian must be provided with much more extensive material related to the data bases themselves. This requires a particularly substantial training effort since any academic community is likely to want access to virtually every data base available on any system—a circumstance that does not apply in most special library situations, where perhaps only three or four data bases are of particular interest.

To meet the greater needs of the academic librarian, NASIC has developed a training program involving both workshops at the NEBHE offices in Wellesley, Massachusetts, and follow-up sessions at the campus of the participating institution. The workshop agenda includes an overview of computerized bibliographic searching and its relationship to traditional reference services, an introduction to the techniques and protocols for searching on one software system, and detailed presentations on five data bases (either in science and engineering or social science disciplines) emphasizing the coverage and characteristics of the data bases and the most effective techniques for searching them. Substantial computer connect time is provided for each participant to allow for practice with the system and to develop familiarity with the data bases. The training staff for the workshop includes a representative of the vendor as well as the NASIC staff members.

The workshop is followed by a visit to each campus by the NASIC information services librarian to provide additional instruction and supervised terminal practice time. Furthermore, each library can send staff to as many such workshops as necessary to obtain access to all desired data bases. Finally, NASIC has scheduled workshops for experienced users, at which ISLs can be introduced to newly available data bases. The training materials developed for these workshops include presentation outlines, transparencies and hard-copy prints of the transparencies, actual user problems turned into demonstration searches, and various other materials related to specific data bases, specific search systems, and general concepts of computerized searching. The NASIC staff has placed particular emphasis on the data-base-related materials, and considerable research effort has been devoted to documenting the coverage, indexing philosophy, vocabulary structure and other components of the various data bases. Comments from both training workshop participants and vendor representatives have underscored the utility of this emphasis.

In addition to the training package, the staff is also developing a multisystem, multi-data-base NASIC user manual that will be available to library personnel as a reference tool for the conduct of computerized searches. This manual will include brief reviews of system procedures and protocols, descriptions of computerized data bases and their relationships to printed indexes, matrices of searchable data elements, descriptions of common problems of particular systems and data bases and the most effective solutions to these problems, and possibly a correlative index of systems, data bases, and subject areas.

A noteworthy benefit of the development of the NASIC user manual has been the feedback from the NASIC staff to the vendors. In effect, the NASIC staff is performing an analysis of each of the two on-line software systems from the perspective of the user, and the outcome has been the discovery of previously unperceived system capabilities as well as system bugs. Insofar as the latter will lead to software improvements, NASIC will have performed a service useful to the vendor and user alike.

The second area of NASIC activity is concerned with consultative assistance to university libraries in initiating computer searching operations.

The "Guide to Implementation of NASIC Services" is the basic tool used to aid library administrators in the decision-making process related to delivery of machine-readable information services. A meeting is held at each institution implementing NASIC computer search services to discuss the issues of organization, staffing, training, service promotion, accounting, data collection, etc. The library directors of participating institutions have reported that these meetings have been helpful to them by enabling each library to benefit from the experience of others and from that of the NASIC staff. Thus, potentially difficult problems, such as equipment acquisition and determination of pricing policies, can be isolated and faced before they have a negative or delaying impact on service initiation. Also of significant benefit has been the distribution of model forms for service provision, which has eliminated much of the paperwork associated with initiating a new library service.

As indicated earlier, an important component of the successful introduction of computer-based search services on a campus is the effort directed toward user education. NASIC personnel have visited each of the affiliated institutions for day-long sessions at which demonstrations of computerized search services have been provided to faculty and students in the science, engineering and social science departments on campus. These demonstrations have enabled libraries to acquaint their users with one of the newest applications of technology in the information field and to publicize the availability of this new service in the local library, all at no cost to the library as a result of the agreements negotiated by NASIC with the commercial vendors of these services.

A fourth activity of NASIC, covered under the term *negotiation*, relates to NASIC acting as a spokesman for its participating institutions—and, indeed, the academic community as a whole—in dealings with data base producers and computer search vendors. One producer, for example, eliminated for academic users the front-end charge for access to its on-line data base after the NASIC management had pointed out the disadvantages to both producers and users resulting from the imposition of that kind of charge. I think it is also fair to say that NASIC has made the search service vendors more aware of the distinct needs of the academic ISL.

Also in this area has been the negotiation of contracts with the two primary vendors of on-line search services. In general, each agreement provides NASIC with assistance in its training activity through free computer connect time and the time of the supplier's training staff and in the marketing activity through additional free computer time. While the monetary value of these considerations is limited, they do enable NASIC to provide more effective service to its affiliated institutions and thus improve the likelihood of more widespread participation in the program.

It is these negotiated considerations, as well as the experience and expertise of the NASIC staff, that underlie the success of the program to date. Indeed, several libraries already holding contracts with one or more of the vendors have switched their contracts to NASIC to take advantage of the "value added" components associated with NASIC participation. The two major vendors have allowed and often encouraged universities to obtain search services through NASIC because they perceive that NASIC institutions are likely—or have already begun—to make more intensive use of the systems than the universities that have signed direct contracts. This represents an important perception that the existence of NASIC-like intermediaries is of benefit to the supplier as well as to the academic library.

The fifth NASIC activity, that of technical facilitation, is still in the potential stage. The intent here is to use an existing regional computer communications network, most likely that of the New England Regional Computing Program (NERComP), to implement the actual brokerage of information services. The plan is to buy services in bulk (unlimited use at a fixed monthly cost) and to retail these services via the network to participating institutions on an as-needed basis. While the technical capability of the network to undertake this activity will exist in a few months, the barrier to implementation is the process of negotiation with one or more vendors to arrange for guaranteed revenue/unlimited use contracts, which is necessary if the true brokerage mode is to be viable.

This package of "value added" services has been an important factor in initiating machine-readable searching into academic libraries, both as a marketing device to persuade universities to adopt the service and as an aid to encouraging more effective service delivery. Based on our experience to date, I do not think it unfair or immodest to say that NASIC has demonstrated that there is a role for the organizational intermediary in the provision of computerized bibliographic search services.

THE FUTURE OF THE INTERMEDIARY

There is no question in my mind that there will continue to be a need for the trained and experienced person to serve as an intermediary between the end user and the bibliographic information available via computer search systems. While a few regular users will access these systems directly, the great bulk of searching will be done by an intermediary, at least in the foreseeable future.

In the academic environment—and for the most part in the governmental and commercial sector as well—the library will continue to be the most appropriate service delivery location and the role of the ISL will become firmly established. Furthermore, I anticipate an expansion of the library's user education and promotion activities as experience demonstrates that such efforts lead to more intensive and more effective use of computer-based search services.

The future of NASIC and other NASIC-type organizations is not so well assured, however. At least part of NASIC's success can be attributed to a program policy of providing "value added" services at no additional cost to the participating institutions. This policy is based on two premises. The first is NEBHE's position that the purpose of the grant from NSF was to implement the provision of machine-readable search services at the colleges and universities of the region and that grant funds should be expended to aid in this implementation process. Furthermore, since pledges of institutional cooperation were a prerequisite to obtaining the grant, it is only fair to distribute the benefits of the NSF funding among the participating institutions. The second premise underlying the provision of "value added" services at no charge is based on pragmatic considerations. Since each of the major vendors sells services on a no-subscription, no-monthly-minimum basis, it would have been very difficult to persuade institutions to obtain services under NASIC auspices if doing so would have entailed a subscription fee. The demise of the Science Information Association, which provided intermediary services on a subscription basis, offers evidence to support this conclusion. Even if institutions did perceive the value of intermediary services and were willing to pay a subscription fee, the absence of demonstrated capability by the NASIC program would have discouraged initial institutional support for the program.

NASIC's mandate from NSF is to assist the universities of the region in developing and implementing local search service capabilities. This development process requires substantial funding, and it is for this purpose that NSF provided the NASIC grant to NEBHE. By the time the NSF funding is exhausted (probably the end of June 1976), it is projected that NASIC will have assisted all Northeast academic institutions desiring to provide search services under NASIC auspices.

The tasks of an ongoing NASIC will be significantly fewer than those in the development phase. The training will be primarily of a continuing education sort, with emphasis on new data bases as they become available. Materials development will concentrate on the updating of documents already produced. User education and negotiation with vendors will continue to be important activities, but there will be far less administrative liaison with participating institutions. We presently estimate that a professional staff of one person at full-time and a second at one-fourth- to one-half-time, along with a half-time secretary, will be sufficient for an ongoing NASIC program. The cost of such a program would be $50,000-$60,000 per year.

Where will this money come from? The primary source will have to be institutional support. With an anticipated thirty to thirty-five participating universities, each institution probably will not have to pay more than $1,000-$2,000 per year, based on volume of system use.

The willingness of the institutions to commit funds to underwrite the intermediary role of NASIC will depend on many factors, including their perception of the quality of service provided by the NASIC staff. However, the major justification for such support clearly will lie in the financial benefits NASIC will have negotiated with the vendors. The greater the benefits, the greater the likelihood of institutional support. The present package of free computer time for training and service demonstrations appears to be an absolute minimum—and perhaps not enough.

NASIC has demonstrated success in signing up academic users and in creating more intensive use of computerized search services by existing academic customers, i.e., in increasing the revenue flowing to the service vendors. From the vendors' perspective, NASIC has functioned effectively and at very little cost as a marketing agent. An ongoing NASIC will continue to provide these benefits to the vendors, which implies that the survival of NASIC is in the vendors' interest.

The vendors can assist in assuring the survival of NASIC in two ways. The first is to negotiate an agreement whereby the vendors recognize the value of the training and marketing services provided by NASIC and compensate NASIC in the form of rebates which can be passed along to the participating institutions. This kind of savings would assure institutional support for NASIC and, if the savings were passed along to the users, would lead to more intensive system use and, thus, to ultimately greater revenues for the vendors.

The second means by which the vendors can facilitate the survival of NASIC is through direct monetary compensation for training and marketing services rendered. Any revenues so obtained would decrease the sums required from the institutions and would thus increase the probability of institutional willingness to support an ongoing NASIC.

Although I have been discussing the future of the intermediary organization specifically in terms of NASIC, the problems faced by our program are no different from those that would have to be overcome by any organization attempting to play an intermediary role in the delivery of computer-based reference services. While there is no doubt in my mind that the activities of NASIC-like organizations are of benefit to academic libraries, to service vendors and, most importantly, to users, the ultimate test of their utility lies in the willingness of those benefiting to underwrite the program. The success or failure of NASIC in this test will be of great interest not only to the National Science Foundation but to other organizations, both public and private-for-profit, that might consider undertaking an intermediary role. And, insofar as this role does have an effect on the use of machine-readable bibliographic services, the results of this test will also have a long-term impact on the use of scientific and technical information in American society.

APPENDIX

NASIC-Affiliated Institutions, 1974-75

Columbia University

Dartmouth College

Harvard University

Massachusetts Institute of Technology

New York Institute of Technology

Northeastern University

Plymouth State College

Princeton University

Tufts University

University of Connecticut

University of Delaware

University of Massachusetts/Amherst

University of Massachusetts/Worcester

University of New Hampshire

University of Pennsylvania

University of Rhode Island

Worcester Polytechnic Institute

Yale University

ROGER K. SUMMIT
Manager
Information Systems Programs
Lockheed Research Laboratory
Palo Alto, California
and
SALLY J. DREW
Director
Task Force on Interlibrary Cooperation and Resource Sharing
Division for Library Services
Wisconsin

The Public Library As An Information Dissemination Center: An Experiment In Information Retrieval Services For The General Public

A decade ago, on-line access to large bibliographic data bases was restricted to large governmental organizations that had the financial assets needed to prepare large data bases and to access them in an efficient manner. As a result of reduced computer and communications costs, this access broadened to industrial users and to universities over the past several years[1] and now, finally, an experiment is being conducted which brings such access directly to the public through the public library system. If the use of on-line services for reference retrieval is to continue to grow, the next potential user group is the general public who, in fact, paid for much of the creation of these data bases through taxes. It is appropriate that an attempt be made to allow the general public to benefit from the vast research and development expenditures of the 1960s through convenient computer access to these files of bibliographic material. The first part of this paper summarizes the experiment to date; the second part provides individualized insight into its operation through the eyes of one of the participating librarians in the study.

THE DIALIB EXPERIMENT
Roger K. Summit

As the result of a proposal by the Lockheed Information Systems Program Office, a two-year experiment has been established by the Office of Science Information Service (OSIS) of the National Science Foundation (NSF). The purpose of this study, called DIALIB, is to probe the utility of the public library as a "linking agent" to the many machine-readable data bases now available. Because individuals and small organizations are unable to afford the cost of a computer terminal ($3000-$5000 purchase cost, $100-$175 monthly rental) and the attendant training in the access language, the public library appears to be an attractive potential institution to service the general public in this regard. At the same time, the study allows the library to experiment with a powerful new technology. The basic questions investigated in the study are: Is computerized retrieval of use to the general public? Will the public be willing to pay to defray part or all of the cost? What impact will retrieval terminals have on the public as well as on the library?

For the first year of operation, the terminals, search time and demonstration time are available at no cost to the libraries in order to familiarize the library staff with on-line retrieval and to determine whether the service is of use to the public. The libraries pay the telephone line charges. For the second year of operation, the terminals and demonstration time are again provided free, but a portion of the cost of the search time is billed to the libraries, with the NSF paying the balance. Some combination of internal library budget and patron fees could be used to meet these costs. By the third year of operation, the library will be expected to pay for the full cost of the terminals and search time.

The Cooperative Information Network (CIN), an information-sharing cooperative in the San Francisco Bay area consisting of both private and public libraries, selected the public libraries that were to participate, and the Lockheed Information System provided the project direction and the DIALOG on-line retrieval service.[2] The study is being evaluated by Applied Communications Research (ACR) of Palo Alto, California, an independent evaluation subcontractor.

In June 1974, CIN selected four libraries for the terminal locations, with each library representing a somewhat different type of library service: a large city library (San Jose Public Library), a county library in a suburban area (Santa Clara County library, Cupertino), a county library with no walk-in traffic (San Mateo County library, Belmont), and a smaller city library with much walk-in business (Redwood City Public Library).

Librarians from each of the four participating libraries were given a two-day training course at Lockheed, and spent about one month familiarizing themselves with the system. A large amount of publicity was generated by the official opening ceremonies in August 1974, and diverse promotional materials were developed. In addition, the participating libraries publicized availability of the retrieval service by demonstrations held in various branch libraries and at meetings of professional and social organizations. A portable terminal was shared for this purpose. Actual productive searching began in September 1974.

Search Mechanics

Libraries utilize the G. E. Terminet terminal, a relatively quiet, impact print, 30 characters-per-second terminal. The terminal is acoustically coupled on a dial-up basis to some twenty-three data bases stored on the Lockheed/ DIALOG computer. In total, these data bases comprise over 6 billion bytes of storage and more than 6 million bibliographic references and abstracts in a multitude of disciplines and specialty areas.

Searching is accomplished using the DIALOG on-line retrieval language which has been described elsewhere[3] and is summarized in the Appendix. Basically, the searcher describes the topic to be searched as Boolean lists of keywords and/or descriptors. Because the indexes and thesauri can be displayed on-line, the user can quickly determine candidate terms for a given topic. The iterative nature of the language allows the user to build his search one step at a time, with feedback from the computer at every step to assist him to define his query more effectively.

Experience to Date

Table 1 indicates the totals for several measured statistics for March 1975—the latest month for which figures are available at this writing.

One of the most striking aspects of these statistics is the wide variation from library to library. For example, San Mateo County required an average of ten minutes of on-line time per search, while Santa Clara County required thirty-six minutes per search. Some of the factors that can cause such differences are: (1) presence or absence of the patron at the time of the search, (2) the training and experience of the librarian, (3) the attitude of the librarian toward the system, (4) whether the request is from a branch library or directly from a patron, and (5) differences in types of questions due to differences in the interests of patrons from region to region. These factors will

	San Mateo County	Redwood City	San Jose	Santa Clara County
Number of searches	66	70	50	42
Number of search hours	10.5	20.0	21.0	25.0
Total hours required librarian time	31.1	34.0	30.4	48.7
Time/search	9.6 min.	17.1 min.	25.2 min.	36.0 min.
Off-line time/search	16 min.	6 min.	11 min.	33 min.

Table 1. Search Statistics for March 1975

Psychology

Child abuse
Meditation
Art therapy
Behavioral approaches to counseling
Mental health
Behavior therapy/marriage

Education

Accreditation
Learning disabilities
Bilingual education
Parent participators
Science instruction

Biology/Medicine

Abiogenesis
Cellulose from protein
Protein gel
Cocaine
Antibiotics
Rh incompatibility

Law

Crime and theories of gun control
Parliamentary law

Engineering/Science

Computerized data banks
Mining
Associative memories-computers
Thin film magnetic tapes
Computer output microfilm
Boat building industry
Plastics processing
Hydrogen production
Concrete water tanks
Ion-beam processing
Auger spectroscopy
Microspheres
Natural gas
Hydrogen production
Parabolic antenna

Social Services/Government

Recycling paper
Technology transfer
Noise pollution
Speaker credibility
Zero population growth

Agricultural

Cattle feed—algae
Rabbit breeding
Growing bananas

Figure 1. Typical Search Topics Grouped by General Category

be evaluated in future ACR reports, and an attempt will be made to relate them to search effectiveness as evidenced by patron satisfaction.[4]

Search questions cover a variety of topics, as shown in Figure 1. As a result, the experiment seems to be having substantial impact on the public, the libraries, and the staff. The public tends to be highly educated, and to use the service for job-related activities (professionals) or for research papers (students). The libraries find that they are reaching a substantial group of former nonusers as well as some established users.

Most of the librarians have quickly adapted to the use of the terminal. They react differently, however, both to the large number of patrons attracted to the service, and to the more demanding nature of this new class of patron. Such patrons can require more of the reference librarian's time, and are often more critical of the results than the typical reference patron.

First Year Conclusions

The first year of the project has shown that computerized search allows the public library to offer in-depth search service in diverse intellectual fields, and in fields in which the reference librarian is not expert. Computerized reference retrieval has been of great use to the public libraries that do not have a large reference collection. It also can be more cost effective than manual search for many topic areas even when a large reference collection is available. The public has shown great interest in the service and has expressed very positive evaluations of the results obtained. We anxiously await the second year, which will demonstrate whether or not the public is willing to pay for such services.

ONE LIBRARIAN'S EXPERIENCE
Sally J. Drew

The Redwood City Public Library has been deeply involved in the DIALOG project for the past ten months. The computer terminal, located in the reference room, has a large sign above it visually describing the service. Curiosity prompts many patrons to ask about the service; and when the terminal is in operation, people often request an explanation, turning many searches into demonstrations as well. The patron is encouraged to be present at the time of the search, but this is not always possible.

Initially, most patrons came from the vicinity of Redwood City. In the last several months, however, we have been receiving many requests from

At the time of the conference, Sally J. Drew was Supervisor of Reference Services at the Redwood City Public Library, Redwood City, California.

outside the area. Patrons come in or mail requests from Stanford University, the College of San Mateo, and numerous industries in surrounding communities. Some searches are requested at neighboring public libraries and then forwarded to us.

Search Experiences

The introduction of DIALOG as a reference tool affects reference service in a variety of ways. Access to these additional data bases greatly extends our abilities to provide information in the area of science and technology, education, and the social sciences.

For example. a product designer sought information on the patent status, methods of manufacturing, various uses and production costs of microspheres. Ordinarily, this patron would have been referred to the *Applied Science and Technology Index* where we might have located a few citations. Instead, a DIALOG search was done while he was there, and almost fifty citations were uncovered, including information on manufacturing processes, product uses, and production problems and costs. Although we did not find the present status of patents, we did learn the name of the firm currently involved in research and production of this product.

Another patron wanted to investigate a variety of topics, including the effects of overprotection of children and the phenomenon of gifted children who are academic underachievers. At another time, an allergist asked for information concerning high efficiency air circulation. He had been working on a new type of indoor air filter, and before going any further, needed to know what other research was currently being carried out in that field. The first search led to a number of others in related areas and proved very valuable. This particular set of searches also expanded library capabilities in tracking down source materials. A patron who taught a course at Stanford University located a few of the source documents in Stanford's collection. Then he returned to us, and we borrowed many of the NTIS research reports from the California State Library.

Over the last ten months, we have tackled questions in other technical areas including the process of underground coal gasification, the effect of aircraft noise on the learning patterns of school children, and the health hazards of using polyvinyl chloride in plastic pipes.

Usage Patterns

The addition of DIALOG has had a definite impact on the range of reference work we can successfully carry out, and we feel it has expanded the variety of people using our services. Studies conducted by Applied Communications Research show some definite trends: the average

DIALOG user is highly educated—over 80 percent are college graduates, and 40 percent have advanced degrees. The two principal user classes are: (1) technical professionals, including civil, nuclear, and electronic engineers, geologists, and computer specialists, and (2) students at all levels. The next two major user categories are: (1) individuals in educational fields, teachers, professors, and school administrators, and (2) librarians. Other frequent users include lawyers, doctors and local government personnel. Patrons say they request searches in order to get information for job-related activities or for research papers.[5]

There is evidence that many DIALOG users are not necessarily traditional library users. In response to a questionnaire, a large number of patrons indicated that they do not have a card at a local public library. Twenty-nine percent of Redwood City DIALOG users say they use the library reference service several times or more each month, while approximately 53 percent use it only several times a year or not at all. Some of these patrons are discovering the diverse resources of the public library for the first time. Not only are they unaware of the quality of reference service available, but they also do not know that the library circulates records, art prints, films, and nonprint materials.

DIALOG has shown a potential for broadening the base of library support in another way. City and county employees and administrators have shown increased interest in the library. They have requested searches on subjects such as technology transfer, solar energy, helicopter noise levels, and open-channel flow of storm waters.

Problems and Challenges

There are pros and cons to all new projects, and DIALOG has imposed stress on our reference services. We are not providing any extra staffing for this project and since June 1974 we have carried out 450 searches and the professional workload has increased by about twenty hours per week. This has stretched an already overcrowded schedule to the limit, and a few of the more traditional activities such as collection development have suffered. If the flow of requests remains steady, additional staff time must be added to account for extra workload.

Inadequate communication between the patron and librarian, an age-old problem, has surfaced again with new dimensions. Patrons often have trouble explaining the exact nature of their requests, and this is compounded when they are asked to supply precise keywords as well as a general description of the topic to be searched. It is important that the patron take part in developing a search strategy in order to understand fully how the results are obtained. The patron's presence at the time of the search offers some advantages. Being more familiar with the subject matter than the librarian, the patron can scan terms listed in the on-line thesaurus and reject or accept them as the search progresses. This provides maximum interaction between patron and librarian but is often more costly, since the patron is charged for time spent in conversation and consultation. Patrons are often somewhat confused by the search process and demand explanations, further increasing the length of time and thus the cost, spent on a search. However, when a search produces few or no citations, the patron's presence increases his understanding of these negative results. Balancing all these factors becomes very important when developing a search strategy which provides the best results for the least expense.

Computer searches sometimes retrieve irrelevant citations through no real fault of the operator. One search on the relation of diet, nutrition, and food to cancer retrieved several abstracts which discussed the potential development of the cancer crab as a food source; all other citations were right on target.

Defining the scope of a search can cause misunderstanding. After receiving the results of a very thorough search on the subject of person perception, a patron called back and requested further material on person perception of blacks. Because the librarian had pulled all citations including the term "person perception," there was little use in repeating the narrower form of the search. The results would have been in a slightly neater package, but no new citations would have been produced without a change in search terms.

Explaining the content of the data bases and the range of information they contain is a continuous process. Dissatisfaction with a search is often the result of seeking information about a subject on which little current research is available or in an area not covered by the abstract services offered. People must constantly be reminded that this form of computer service will not answer an exact question, such as, "How many people in the United States hold credit cards?" but will instead supply a list of articles discussing credit card use by Americans.

The confrontation between computer and public often has a humorous twist. Many people have an overwhelming confidence that the computer can solve their problems. While it is discouragingly ready to accept the inability of the librarian to provide an instant answer, the public finds it hard to believe that the computer cannot provide an instant, definitive response. This breeds an interesting form of paranoia. Some patrons feel that the material they want is in the computer, but the operator is too incompetent to find it, or that the wrong subject headings were used to describe the alleged articles which will satisfy all of their needs.

One problem which we expected to be paramount—but which did not actually materialize—is the locating of source documents. Our affiliation with the Cooperative Information Network helps us to track down sources for documents, and the California State Library provides others. Many patrons seem satisfied with the citations or abstracts provided, and others locate source materials on their own.

Up to now, the public has shown a great deal of enthusiasm for this project. There is no doubt that if this service were incorporated into regular library service on a free basis, many people would use it. On the other hand, it is questionable whether the public library can afford to do this. Taxpayers generally are not predisposed to shower money on their public institutions in these hard times. Librarians now have to defend current programs against budget cuts. It seems unlikely that the vast amounts of money needed to support computerized literature searching will be provided from traditional sources of revenue in the near future.

Therefore, DIALOG will probably have to become self-supporting and the second year of the project will test this possibility. The prospect of charging patrons for service has always raised many questions among librarians. The many arguments for and against it are outside the scope of this discussion, however. There is also no doubt that charging will add different dimensions to library service; it will change the librarian/patron relationship, and negotiating the answer to some kinds of questions may well take on new dimensions. Patrons will tend to be increasingly demanding about the quality of service. Charging for DIALOG will force administrative policy changes and place additional burdens on other departments. For example, the circulation desk will have to deal with greater sums of money, deposits, and fees, and with issuing receipts.

The largest question is still whether the patron will pay for this type of service. Analysis of the characteristics of DIALOG users indicates that they probably can afford to pay, but will they be willing to? Americans seem to hold the assumption that information has always been and should be free. This has not always been true, but it is still a powerful influence on people's thinking and habits. Whether these habits can be redirected remains debatable. It is hoped that data from the second half of this experiment will provide some direction for future policy.

REFERENCES

1.   Summit, Roger K., and Firschein, Oscar. "Document Retrieval Systems and Techniques." *In* Carlos A. Cuadra and Ann W. Luke, eds. *Annual*

Review of Information Science and Technology. Vol. 9. Washington, D. C., American Society for Information Science, 1974, pp. 285-331.

    2.   Summit, Roger K. "DIALOG Interactive Information Retrieval System." *In* Allen Kent and Harold Lancour, eds. *Encyclopedia of Library and Information Science*. Vol. 7. New York, Marcel Dekker, 1972, pp. 161-69.

    3.   *Ibid.*

    4.   Ahlgren, Alice E. "Factors Affecting the Adoption of an Online Service by the Public Library." Paper presented at the 4th ASIS Mid-Year Meeting, Portland, Oregon, May 15-17, 1975.

    5.   *Ibid.*

APPENDIX A

The DIALOG Retrieval System

DIALOG is an interactive, computer-based information retrieval language developed at the Lockheed Palo Alto Research Laboratory, consisting of a series of computer programs designed to make full use of direct-access memory devices (in which data located anywhere on the device can be accessed in approximately the same amount of time) and display units to provide the user with a rapid and powerful means of identifying records within a file that satisfy a particular information need. By providing the user full display access to the indexing vocabulary and enabling him to modify search expressions, DIALOG becomes a data processing extension of the human operator who directs and controls the process.

The user issues commands to the computer via a keyboard, and receives results on the display unit. DIALOG allows the user with a well-defined search topic to proceed directly to desired records; the user who cannot explicitly define his requirement is provided with tools for browsing through the file. It is thus possible to investigate successive avenues of interest as they arise or are suggested by intermediate retrieval results.

The search process is broken up into a sequence of small steps, each of which is very simple, and each of which results in feedback from the system. In this manner, each step is completed correctly before proceeding, thus eliminating the need to reenter the entire search specification in case of error. Following are some of the commands available to the user.

EXPAND—This command provides a display of the alphabetically close index terms relative to the term entered. The number of citations indexed by the displayed term is also given. This feature eliminates the problem of variant spellings or of singular and plural forms; e.g., expanding *computer*, one can readily select additional terms such as *computers* and *computing* from the display. This command can also be used to obtain conceptually related terms for those data bases having a stored thesaurus.

SELECT—This command results in the definition of file subsets (referred to as "sets") which are tagged with "set numbers" and are printed out on the terminal hard-copy device.

COMBINE—This allows the searcher to combine any number of citation sets using the logical relationships AND, OR, and NOT. Thus, *digital* and *computers* will form the set of citations containing the term *digital* as well as the term *computers*, while *digital* OR *computers* will form the set of citations that satisfy either *digital*, or *computers*, or both.

DISPLAY—The DISPLAY command allows the user to review intermediate results in various formats. The most frequently used format provides a display of the entire citation, including all assigned descriptors and a descriptive abstract if available. Supplying the full citation not only enables the user to evaluate the relevancy of his search to that point, but it also shows alternative descriptors that he can explore or include (using the COMBINE command) with other previously developed categories.

PRINT—This command allows the user to obtain listings of desired citations in an off-line mode. Prints are prepared on the high-speed printer and mailed to the user.

Although this basic set of five commands will enable the user to perform useful searches, additional commands such as the "full text" commands (allowing all nontrivial words in the title and abstract to be treated as search terms) provide the user with additional search power and flexibility.

The DIALOG system is run on an IBM 360/65 computer having one million bytes of core storage. The direct access memory consists of one billion bytes of disk memory (IBM 3330 equivalent) and 4½ billion bytes of data-cell memory. Input to the system is via multiple ports consisting of high-speed leased lines (480 characters per second), direct-dialed lines (30 cps or 120 cps), TYMSHARE lines (30 cps), and a TWX port (10 cps). The IBM operating systems are used to control the system, and the DIALOG retrieval software is written in assembly language, while many of the file preparation and accounting programs are written in PL/I.

KENNETH E. DOWLIN
Director
Pikes Peak Regional Library District
Colorado Springs, Colorado
and
ELISABETH FULLER
Acting Director
Natrona County Public Library
Casper, Wyoming

Community Information Center: Talk Or Action?

How do you change a nice, traditional library into a community information center? The literature is full of bright ideas, but a mere facelift will not do it. We must change our image, provide rapid information services, use visual and other media, and use the computer. This presentation concerns itself mainly with the computer.

Several factors make computers viable in smaller libraries: data bases are smaller, smaller and cheaper hardware is now available and most libraries have access to it, communities have a great need for sophisticated information retrieval methodology, our traditional methods are too slow and prone to error, society is attuned to the tempo of television rather than that of books, the growth of regional and national machine-readable data bases requires local systems for maximum effectiveness and, to develop true rapid information systems, we need local data processing capabilities.

The Natrona County Public Library (NCPL) could not afford the hardware and systems development required to implement an on-line system. In order to do this it had to expand its mass. It needed to reach the critical mass

This material was presented in video form at the conference.

to obtain the capabilities. This could be done by expanding geographically or by expanding functions. The most feasible way of expansion was by function. First, the library undertook a contract to develop information systems for county offices; later, it contracted with the local school district to share a computer. We called this project the County Records System (CRS).

The CRS was formulated to meet two major goals: (1) to develop local expertise and hardware to provide microfilming of records in county offices for archival, security, and rapid access purposes; and (2) to develop in the Natrona County Public Library the expertise and the hardware to use microfilm and computer technology for the provision of information services.

The program was separately funded by the county commissioners, and in the first year approximately $40,000 was spent for operations. A considerable amount of this was spent on staff and training. An additional $41,000 was spent on equipment. The second fiscal year is budgeted at $48,000 for operations and $18,000 for equipment. The funds budgeted for the equipment include funds for leasing an NCR-101 computer for eight hours each day from the Natrona County School District. It is anticipated that continued funding will be provided by the County Commissioners. As county office back files are microfilmed and indexed, the cost of the operation should decline; nevertheless, we have found that as we complete one phase, a new project occurs.

Our County Records System consists of a filming operation and an indexing system. Filming is done primarily on a Kodak Reliant 700 (rotary); we have a Kodak MRD II and a Kodak portable. At this time all of our filming is done in 16mm. We develop our own film, quality check it, and process it into the required format (e.g., microfiche). Indexing may be as simple as a label or as complex as a computer-generated printout, depending upon each office's needs. If a computer index is generated, the printout will also be filmed and diazo copies made available.

The indexing system is built around a master record (95 characters or extended up to 480 characters). Each record is composed of fields which may be localized to modify the master record according to individual office applications. By programming and manipulating the master record in modules, the index system is interlocked step by step; each step uses components of the previous step. Since the fields can be modified, we do not need to reprogram from scratch for every index designed.

The initial barrier to creating the index system was our computer's central processing unit (CPU). It has a capacity of only 16K. This limitation prohibited the use of package systems, such as those of NCR or IBM, for rapid access to the disc files. We therefore structured our own file, filing the records alphabetically in indexed buckets. We estimate that our run time is longer than that required by a virtual storage system, since each inquiry has more steps. However, this is not a problem at present since the computer is available for a considerable length of time.

It is anticipated that as the system grows—particularly if we start using terminals for on-line indexing—we will need a CPU with at least 48K. At that point, the file structure might be transferred into a package system to speed up access time.

At the end of the first eighteen months of operation, the system has developed in many respects. The sheriff's office is completely filmed and operating on an up-to-date basis. The probate files at the clerk of the district court are filmed and are on an up-to-date basis (these files are about one-third of the total for that office). Civil court files are currently being filmed. We have filmed, on a project basis, records of the county treasurer, and we have filmed and computerized the license plate records. The county clerk has our proposal to use aperture cards and security reels in his office and we are testing the procedures; we have filmed on a project basis for him, also. The local hospital has asked our advice and assistance with their filming projects.

Details of the system vary according to the particular application. In the sheriff's office, we filmed a four-year backlog and are now on an update basis for the arrest, call and license plate registration files. Everything pertinent to the record is filmed, including mug shots and fingerprints, although they may be maintained in separate files for daily use. The update is filmed once a week and includes all material accumulated during the week. The material is organized and coded for existing location and offense by the sheriff's staff. Our camera crew films it on the Kodak Reliant 700 in an auxiliary film unit. Thus, the film can be exposed at a scheduled time, instead of waiting until an entire reel has been filmed on the main film unit. The auxiliary film unit contains a partial reel, which is cut as used for catch-up filming. The film is processed, inspected for quality and loaded into micro-fiche jackets.

Record of a new arrest is allocated one channel, unless there are more than thirteen items. Updates for previous arrest records are added to the channel or treated as overflow materials. Provisions have been made for overflow records: either the next channel is allocated or a cross reference location is added to the computer index of the channel used. Records of calls made to the sheriff's office are generally not updated, so they are packed into the channels at a rate of approximately eight call sheets per channel. License plate registrations are also packed, at approximately thirteen to a channel.

Each jacket is labeled and then duplicated on a diazo printer/processor. The diazos are loaded into retrieval cartridges and routed to the keypuncher. The jackets are filed in the CRS work area for security and possible updates.

The keypunch operator has a Bruning model 95 microfiche cartridge retrieval unit on which to display the diazos; this machine is a twin of the unit used by the sheriff's office. The operator locates each record and keypunches the following information from the record itself: name, alias, date, and NCIC offense code. Location in the arrest file or call file is derived from the mechanical buttons on the retrieval unit.

These keypunched cards are read onto discs and arranged in alphabetical sequence using a chained-index sequential file based on buckets. (The buckets allow access within five records of the one required, with only one look-up.) The disc files may also be sorted or searched by date, NCIC offense code or, in the future, a property code. The index is created from this file, printed and microfilmed on the Reliant 700. It is then loaded into jackets, diazoed and put into an index cartridge. The index contains much of the information of the record itself, thus providing immediate access for sheriff's office personnel to information as to whether a person has called before, or has been arrested before, when, how often, why, and whether he has used an alias. A property code module has not been implemented, since no suitable code system is available from NCIC. When a coding system becomes available, the sheriff's office will adopt it, adding it to their records. The computer program has a slot already built in—anticipating this information. We are analyzing the system used by the State of Washington for possible use.

The cartridges are delivered to the sheriff's office for permanent storage. (If a record is updated which is in an earlier cartridge, the diazo only is delivered to the office and substituted in the cartridge.) Using the automatic retrieval unit, the sheriff's office personnel first check the index and then, if necessary, go on to the individual record. Only one retrieval unit is currently set up at the office, but a second unit is on order. Since a reader-printer unit is to be developed, none has been purchased as yet. Fortunately, this situation has not proved to be too great a handicap.

Storage of more than one million records was creating severe space limitations at the court clerk's office. By working up file definitions we discovered that the need for accuracy was far more important than rapid access. Thus, a reel film system seemed appropriate. Two reels are filmed at one time; one is the office copy, the other is sent to the state archives in Cheyenne as the security copy.

Indexing, geared to numbered targets separating each case filmed, is done at the time of quality checking after the film is developed. Keypunching is done from index sheets listing the file name, reel number, names, case number, target number, judgment information and date, status, satisfaction, and whether sent to the state supreme court. The cards are read into the computer, sorted and printed alphabetically, then sorted and printed by case number and file. Thus, a one-step search by name is possible, or the case number listing may be used if the alphabetical index system (which does not include the film location) has been the primary look-up.

One complete file has been filmed for the clerk of court within less than one year. Production speed is high—up to 13,000 papers per week. However, a backlog of cases must be prepared by the clerk's staff to maintain this filming rate. Each case must be checked against the docket card, sorted, and missing material located.

A current fiche system to record, by law, the judgments of the court is one of the projects which has utilized camera time when the backlog of cases ready for filming is not enough to keep the film crew busy. Original wills, kept in special books, have been filmed and added to the computer index for the clerk of court.

The county treasurer's tax rolls of a ten-year period were filmed in three weeks to ease space in that office. No computer index was generated for the tax rolls since they were in a numerical sequence; they were simply labeled with the inclusive ledger numbers. Two copies of these films were produced. One was retained by the office and one was sent to the state archives in Cheyenne.

License plate records are filmed numerically. Autos, trucks, and trailers each have a separate file. Film is jacketed, diazoed, and keypunched from the cartirdge format as in the sheriff's office operation. For each plate, the name, number, and file is punched; the cards are then run to produce an alphabetical index. The cartridges go to the sheriff's office along with a filmed copy of the index. The jackets and paper printout belong to the treasurer's office.

We have recently begun designing the county clerk's daily recording and film index system. We plan to use elements of other clerk and recorder systems (security reels and aperture cards) combined with an alphabetical computer index.

Ninety percent of our county clerk's records are on film (done by the state archives department). We have purchased duplicate copies of this film (750 reels). Unfortunately, we will have to verify every filmed record for quality and legibility and, whenever necessary, the record will be refilmed. The film done by the state is on 16mm and 35mm formats. Thus, we will use both 16mm and 35mm aperture cards. The card sizes are the same, but the number of images per card varies: four per 16mm, two per 35mm.

We plan to do current filming on 16mm in two stages: each record will be filmed in the county clerk's office by his personnel. Two reels of film will be exposed at once. One will become a security copy for the state archives; the other will be a working copy retained in the county clerk's office. Records to be put into aperture cards will be refilmed on the Reliant 700. Again, two reels will be filmed; one will be cut up and loaded into aperture cards, and the other will be made available for purchase by abstractors.

The indexing system involves an alphabetical name listing, a daily reception book and, in the future, a tract index arranged by land description.

The name index can be keypunched directly from the microfilmed backfile indexes. Current indexing can be done on computer code sheets and keypunched directly from them. The name index will contain name, date, file and location, and a brief description. The computer can list these in one alphabetical sequence which is not now possible in hand-written index books. The reception book is a numerical list of all instruments handled in the office that day. A tract or abstract index for land description is also planned. This index will be on a very sophisticated level and require a great deal of input time.

We anticipate that this system will save money. Presently, a photostat machine is used to make the records and duplicates for customers. The machine is expensive to operate and difficult to maintain. In the currently proposed system, the records will be on microfilm and customer duplicates can be made from a reader/printer which is cheaper to operate and to maintain.

We worked with the county hospital for several months, designing and discussing a backfile system and a current system. They have nearly decided on the best route to obtain equipment and supplies. They plan to use their own personnel as much as possible. We have offered to work with them in areas of training and film processing. Since the hospital was not included in our original system, they will reimburse us for supplies, etc., which they use.

How do we plan to use this system in the NCPL operation? This question relates to the argument I used to convince the county commissioners to support the CRS program. The library is the only agency in our county government that has the expertise of handling information *and* retrieving it, and we can use the expertise and hardware provided for CRS to handle library functions and other agencies' information needs.

We are in a good position, being a samll library, to computerize. Our hardware, though small, is adequate and our file sizes are manageable. We plan to use the index programming to develop an on-line catalog system. We know that local history sources (diaries and documents) could be microfilmed and indexed. Small appliance and motor manuals belonging to the public could be handily filmed, indexed and returned. We would like to microfilm and index our 6,000 maps for security copies and easy access via our video reference service. We could also experiment with the automatic cartridge retrieval units to retrieve magazine articles. Articles on microfiche loaded in cartridge units, located via the *Reader's Guide Index*, could save a considerable amount of time and headache involved in magazine reference work. We could also interface this magazine file system with the video reference service.

We believe that to meet the primary role of public libraries, which is to provide information services, we must develop the expertise and the hardware to be able to handle high-speed information systems. We have to learn to work with computers and microfilm in addition to the traditional materials in order to provide these information services. I feel that the primary role of a public librarian is to serve as an interface between the public and the informational technology and data bases available today. It gives us the challenge and the opportunity to make public libraries an essential service of governments. We must raise library service to the next plateau. To do this will require a lot of imagination and some guts. At Natrona County Public Library we know where we are going, we know what it will take to get there, and we have started down the road of achieving the goals of information services. Our long-range goal is to be able to answer any question of any patron in a short time. This means that we hope to be able to answer 95 percent of the questions we receive in less than two minutes. This takes a major revision in our philosophy and our operations—but it can be done.

When we undertook this project we had to start from scratch. We found no library agencies to give us systems or hardware support; we have been on our own. This leads us into our second major need: library data processing networks. The network should provide: (1) generalized high-speed communications between all elements of the network, (2) sophisticated data processing capabilities, (3) coordination of the interface of data processing components, (4) sharing of developments in data processing, (5) location of software and, if necessary, its provision, (6) communications to high-level hardware, and (7) standards for interchangeability. We can develop a networking model. There are three underlying assumptions: all libraries may participate at various levels, but they do not have to participate at all; the critical mass for each service can be determined; and people politics is feasible. Figure 1 is a theoretical model of the library data processing network, using cable television to link the library to the user's home.

Using hypothetical minimums for critical mass, our model has these levels:

1. The libraries serve more than 5,000 people or 1,000 students but less than 500,000 people or 10,000 students.
2. The interstate systems serve at least 500,000 people or 10,000 students, but less than 2 million people or 400,000 students.
3. The state agencies serve at least 2 million people or 400,000 students, but less than 10 million people or 2 million students.
4. The multistate library service agencies serve more than 10 million people or 2 million students.

It is obvious that if one library has more than 10 million users, it should be able to provide the services of a multistate library service agency.

A library may go to any level necessary depending on the service. If

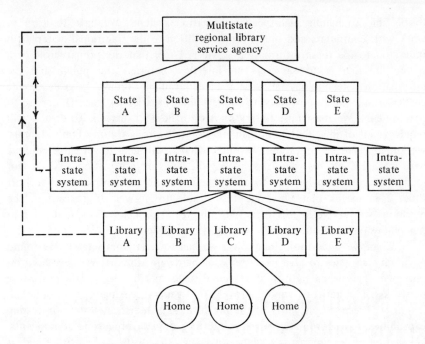

Figure 1. Library Data Processing Network.

clearinghouses are necessary, they may be interposed. We will assume that all elements have terminals that can communicate with each other. A possible service is on-line cataloging and classification. If the critical mass is 2 million, it should be provided by the state library agency. If it requires 10 million, it should be provided by the multistate library agency. If the requirement is 2 million and one library serves that many people, that library should provide the service. The production of cards could require only 500,000 people to be viable. The jacketing of books may only require a base of 5,000. An inventory of area resources could have components at all levels, yet be treated as a whole at the multistate level. The use of commercially produced machine-readable data bases may be tied to any level that has the critical mass for economic viability. Through the communications system it can be available to all elements of the network.

Inventory of local community materials can be done at the local level with spin-offs upward. With the network it should be possible for the library to use short records for inventory purposes, but to rely on the network for full information.

This whole concept is merely an idea. We need the methodology and the impetus to define the critical masses necessary and the mechanics for implementation. We need to raise library science above local, parochial vested interests and plan for an attempt to satisfy our users' information needs.

DAGMAR SCHMIDMAIER
Systems Librarian
University of Sydney Library
Sydney, Australia

Machine-Readable Data Bases In Australia: A State-Of-The-Art Report

This paper aims to present an overview of the use of machine-readable data bases in Australia. (A summary of some commerically available services is given in the Appendix.) I will discuss the Australian scene in the light of some problems which are, if not unique to, certainly aggravated by the Australian environment. These include problems of geography and population distribution, formulation of national information policy, government support of research and development, and the Australian telecommunications network. Plans expounded during the last four years have aroused an unprecedented interest among librarians. Unfortunately, progress to date has been disappointing.

HISTORY AND GEOGRAPHY

Australians look toward the United States and Europe in political and economic affairs, so it is not surprising that the Australian library world behaves in a similar fashion. Librarians look primarily to the United States for new developments.

Australia is geographically isolated. In talking about modern communications and the ease of transporting people from one continent to another, let us not forget that it is a 24-hour flight from Sydney to London and 15 hours from Sydney to the west coast of the United States. Australian librarians do not go to Paris for a two-day seminar as is done with great frequency and enthusiasm in the Northern Hemisphere. Because of our isolation and historical background, Australian librarians feel they are missing out. One of the consequences is a great effort at awareness of overseas developments. This concern can at times be out of proportion and is often expressed in the belief that if systems or concepts are to have any credibility, they must be imported. This is not valid; wholesale importation of systems from a totally foreign environment cannot be accepted without taking account of local conditions.

The population of Australia in 1972 was estimated at 13,091,297, of which 7,132,590 were located in the main cities along the eastern coast.[1] Just as industry and commerce developed in these areas, so did the libraries that support society. Attempts to decentralize have not been successful; for example, colleges of advanced education established outside the metropolitan areas exemplify the problem with their severe lack of resources, particularly qualified, experienced staff. The resources, materials and people are located in twelve major libraries in three capital cities.

THE AUSTRALIAN LIBRARY COMMUNITY

A brief discussion of the structure of the Australian library community is appropriate here. At the federal level is the National Library, which has no statutory supervisory power over any other libraries. The Director General (previously titled the National Librarian) is appointed by cabinet on advice of the Council of the National Library of Australia (NLA). The NLA is responsible for national collection building and, incongruously, for providing local library service to the Canberra community.

At the state level there are reference libraries which differ greatly from each other, in the concept of their function as well as in size. For example, the state library of New South Wales seems more like the National Library than the Queensland State Library. This is due to historical development, since the state libraries (particularly those of New South Wales and Victoria) pursued national policies in their collection building. The state library of New South Wales was the first major collection in Australia, and remains one of our major collections today.

Great variation in the type of organization can also be found at the local government level; for example, library services in New South Wales and Victoria are subsidized by the state on a per capita basis, whereas in Western Australia the state owns the total bookstock. However, development of public libraries has been very slow and the majority have been established only within the last twenty years.

The libraries of educational institutions offer another picture. The majority of primary school libraries are run by the state, while secondary schools are divided sharply into government and private institutions. Government schools are supported by state funds and private schools receive state government subsidies. However, in recent years considerable commonwealth funds have been provided for schools, with libraries receiving a large share. At the tertiary level there are the universities, colleges of advanced education, and technical colleges. All of the universities are independent institutions supported by the commonwealth funds. Since 1958 the universities have been funded directly by the federal government and on a much larger scale than was previously possible. The federal government is the only taxing authority in Australia, there being no direct taxes levied by the states. Over the last few years the federal government has also accepted responsibility for funding the colleges of advanced education and the technical colleges. These were previously administered by state departments of education. Special libraries also cover a wide range, e.g., industrial, business and governmental. In the case of the commonwealth, they are coordinated by their department rather than by the National Library or another central body. In some states the departmental libraries are centrally staffed; for example, in New South Wales the state library is responsible for staff, but does not have authority over departmental library policies.

The library system of the Commonwealth Scientific and Industrial Research Organisation (CSIRO) stands outside these patterns and is an interesting example of a "national" library network. The CSIRO, a statutory corporation operating under its own act of Parliament, is Australia's largest civil scientific body. Its main function is to carry out scientific research for the primary and secondary industries of the commonwealth and its territories. It does not conduct defense, medical or atomic energy research. The CSIRO's Library and Information Service is coordinated centrally and plays a vital role in the Australian library community. Its role as a service center for machine-readable data bases will be discussed later.

Thus we have a picture of library services operating at many different levels and with little overall direction. Development of library resources outside the state library of New South Wales and the libraries of the University of Sydney and the University of Melbourne has occurred since World War II. Together with the NLA, these three libraries hold the major resources of the country. For each type of library—public, university, special, etc.—there are some who have initiated new developments and are leaders in their field, both in traditional methods and in implementation of computer-based systems.

MACHINE-READABLE DATA BASES

Development of machine-readable data bases has therefore been stimulated by the requirements of those libraries' patrons, and while I believe all have attempted to keep an eye on proposed national plans, systems have, of necessity, been established in isolation. Without general guidelines or a national policy there is no alternative. There is, however, some evidence of voluntary cooperation among a few industrial concerns who decided to use the same software package for creating and searching data bases. On the other hand, some government departments developed their own software, and both software and the data base are largely unavailable to the information community because of security problems; examples include systems developed by the Department of Defence (formerly Department of Supply).

Early in the 1960s, the concept of the ADSATIS (Australian Defence Science and Technology Information System) information retrieval system was developed by the library service within the Department of Supply. Considering the remoteness of Australia from other parts of the world where such systems were beginning to appear, the scarcity of hardware and the lack of experience, this was a significant development. The ADSATIS system has developed over the years and is now using COSATI (Committee on Scientific and Technical Information) headings and TEST (Thesaurus of Engineering and Scientific Terms) as the indexing language. ADSATIS is a locally developed system and is used for SDI (selective dissemination of information) and retrospective searching, the majority of the data being classified and unavailable publicly.

As is often the case, the most sophisticated information retrieval systems have been developed within government departments and cannot be used by the information community at large because of their confidentiality. The CSIRO has also developed its own software and is now offering a number of services to the Australian community.

The 1968 survey of computer-based systems in Australian libraries listed twenty-one institutions with a total of thirty-eight "operational" systems. A recent survey indicates that there is a 50 percent increase in both the number of libraries and systems listed.[2] There has been a concurrent significant increase in the number of new libraries, particularly with the establishment of the colleges of advanced education (CAEs), which fill an educational gap between technical colleges and universities. Although funding has been generous, it will be many years before their libraries will be well established. While there has been a slight increase in the number of governmental special libraries, industrial libraries have been hit hard by the economic conditions of the last few years. This overall increase requires a similar increase in the availability of qualified and experienced staff in all areas, particularly in systems and planning. The situation is not totally discouraging because lack of resources does encourage cooperation; it is just not possible for everyone to reinvent the wheel. It does happen of course, but the environment is not encouraging.

Developments in Australia have followed the traditional scheme, i.e., housekeeping systems and information retrieval systems. This pattern tends to emphasize the division by type of library: the former systems are a necessity, and usually the first step for large university, college, and public libraries, whereas information retrieval systems are largely the province of the special library. With all libraries striving to decrease their overall operating costs to reduce the staff budget—which assumes an increasing portion of the total—it seems essential to implement cooperative housekeeping systems. I shall outline some of these developments before discussing information retrieval systems and national information policy.

Victoria leads Australia in the cooperative use of machine-readable data bases; this is largely due to the coexistence of a few librarians with foresight and imagination and an entrepreneur willing to risk capital. A number of public (regional) libraries in Victoria are using a consultant, Libramatic Systems, to provide computerized services. Available systems include acquisitions, cataloging and circulation. This venture is successful because, like the Ohio College Library Center (OCLC), the software allows the participating libraries to vary the standard to suit their local requirements. Unlike OCLC, however, it is a batch processing system with each regional group maintaining a separate data base of its holdings. The bibliographic data base system has been available since 1967 and has developed from a brief fixed format record to a MARC-compatible format. In 1974, the circulation system was upgraded from a punched paper-tape system to an on-line system using bar-coded labels and point-of-sale type terminals for data capture. The new system has been installed in two regional libraries in Victoria and one in New South Wales. The University of Sydney Library is developing its own on-line charging system using the Libramatic terminals and Data General minicomputers. Without doubt, Libramatic Systems has pioneered in the use of computerized systems in Australian libraries. It has introduced operational, efficient and cost-effective systems in the face of extreme scepticism.

It is true that many enthusiastic librarians have had their enthusiasm dampened by reports of failure of heavily funded systems in the United States. However, nourished by success, librarians in Victoria have taken further steps towards cooperation with the formation of TECHNILIB and the Victorian Institute of Colleges Chief Librarians Association (VICCLA). The TECHNILIB committee was formed in 1973 to investigate the feasibility of a centralized processing center for Victorian municipal libraries. VICCLA is an attempt to coordinate developments of CAEs. Both groups are looking toward a central, machine-readable bibliographic data base around which a central processing center can be developed. However, both are still at the planning stage. The use of machine-readable data bases in public and educational libraries is still primarily concerned with the creation of a bibliographic file to be used primarily for card catalog or book catalog production. There has been cooperation in setting up these bibliographic files by exchange of data, systems and programming work.

During 1974, the NLA launched the Australian MARC record service, a landmark in the development of bibliographic data processing. The service began with eight institutions and the NLA as registered users, and provided Library of Congress, British National Bibliography and Australian MARC records. The software was designed and written by Libramatic Systems, who also run the system on behalf of the NLA. Initially, the service offered access only by record control number for each type of record; however, refinements planned will ensure that all records will be available in the Australian MARC format. The use of the MARC data base overseas has to some extent combined the two streams of data base development, in that MARC is used to provide SDI services as well as for inventory control.

It seems that users and creators of information retrieval systems have one tremendous advantage: they are neither burdened by tradition nor necessarily conditioned by the history of librarianship. Consequently, they should be able to adopt a much freer attitude to what computerized systems have to offer. On the other hand, users of library stock control records are very much conditioned by tradition and by their expectations of traditional catalogs, and thus often cannot readily recognize the need for new methods and capabilities.

AN EMERGING NATIONAL INFORMATION POLICY

The 1970s marked the first steps toward establishing a national information policy, with particular emphasis placed on the role of computers. Milestones in this development include: (1) the appointment of the Scientific and Technological Services Enquiry Committee (STISEC) in 1971, (2) government approval of the STISEC recommendations and the establishment of an interdepartmental committee, (3) creation of the Australian National Scientific and Technological Library (ANSTEL) in 1974, and (4) establishment of the Australian Library Based Information System (ALBIS) in 1974.

STISEC

The Scientific and Technological Services Enquiry Committee was appointed by the Council of the National Library in February 1971. Its objectives were: (1) to investigate the national need for scientific and technological information services; and (2) to suggest how, in the national interest, inadequacies identified by its inquiries may be overcome.

The STISEC report, published in May 1973, concluded that there were urgent and growing needs which should be met by coordinating and assisting

existing library and information services and by providing additional services.[3]
The report recommended that the Australian government establish a national
scientific and technological information authority whose functions would be:
(1) promote the orderly development of scientific and technological library
and information services, and (2) to foster the coordination and extension of
existing services, with particular attention given to computer-based information services. The authority should advise on policy development, undertake and support associated research activities, and act as the Australian focus
for international cooperation on the transfer, storage and dissemination of
scientific and technological information. STISEC also urged that information
services in science and technology not be created in isolation, but that they
be integrated into a total information service with the humanities.

This report and subsequent developments have been encouraging because
the government is concerned about formulating a national plan to enable the
future development of library-based information services to be rationalized
and coordinated. The government accepted the committee's recommendations
with only one reservation: the proposed STISEC authority should not be
established as a separate new independent body, but should be within the
framework of the National Library Act. Provision was made for initial
development in fiscal year (FY) 1973/74.

ALBIS

The Australian library world was anticipating clarification of proposed
principles of development of this national service. However, nothing was
forthcoming until an advertisement issued by the NLA burst on a surprised
public in October 1974. It stated that ALBIS was to be based on voluntary
cooperation among federal, state, municipal, industrial, social, academic,
artistic, humanistic, scientific, technological and other organizations able and
willing to contribute to a library-based information system. The needs of the
Australian community would thereby be met by developing traditional and
computer-based services in the most effective way. To achieve this, the
National Library is to undertake extensive consultations and surveys over a
period of two years to determine the feasibility of such a system. To fund
these studies, $1,025,000 has been provided to the National Library.

The library community was unsure about what was really required of it
but responded enthusiastically with more than 200 submissions made to
ALBIS, with 24 percent coming from federal and state bodies, 23 percent
from business and commercial organizations, 15 percent from educational and
university institutions, 13 percent from library associations and libraries, 13
percent from individuals, and 11 percent from associations.

The objectives that such a national system might be expected to meet could be summarized as follows: (1) taking responsibility for providing individuals with the necessary day-to-day information to enjoy the benefits of society, (2) meeting the professional and business needs of individuals and groups in the community, including specialized groups, (3) rationalizing development to avoid overlap in acquisition, maintenance and provision of information services, and (4) ensuring that the development of information services remains in line with developments in electronic and communication technologies. To meet these objectives, the information needs and user requirements must be defined, quantified and evaluated. In addition, computer and telecommunications requirements should be established and costed. ALBIS has been declared alive, but Australian librarians are still going through mental gymnastics in an attempt to find those promised guidelines of leadership and inspiration.

I have taken some time to attempt to analyze this situation, because the formulation of a national information system has been the basis of our thinking for the last few years. Librarians in Australia have been attempting to coordinate their developments in line with this imminent national policy. However, it is difficult to identify with something as intangible as ALBIS.

Until recently the National Library has been the focal point for the development of services from machine-readable data bases. Major developments have been: the introduction of the Australian MEDLARS service in 1969; the 1972 design of the ANB/MARC system to create Australian MARC records for newly published monographs and to automate the production of the Australian National Bibliography; implementation of a pilot project for SDI services from ERIC during 1972/73; introduction of ERIC on an operational basis in 1974; expansion of the biomedical information services in 1974 with the introduction of *BA Previews*; and introduction of the Australian MARC record service in 1974. Moreover, the National Library is the central agency for Australian involvement in a number of activities, including the Australian national focus for UNISIST, the distribution center for MARC records, and the national agency for ISBN/ISSN/ISDS.

CENTRALIZED SCIENTIFIC INFORMATION RESEARCH ORGANIZATION: A DE FACTO NATIONAL INFORMATION SERVICE?

In the light of the developments outlined, it is not surprising that alternative services have sprung up. The CSIRO (Commonwealth Scientific & Industrial Research Organisation) has emerged as an alternate national focus for maintaining and running SDI and retrospective search services.

The function of CSIRO as defined in the Science and Industry Research

Act of 1949 is to further and encourage research in Australia. More specifically, it is entrusted with the "collection and dissemination of information relating to scientific and technical matters; and publication of scientific and technical reports, periodicals and papers."[4] The services offered by CSIRO, which include CA CONDENSATES, INSPEC, *BA Previews* and *Food Science and Technology Abstracts,* are an extension of those developed for its own clientele, and are now being actively marketed for the Australian community at large.

Lack of resources has hampered progress in Australia and the establishment of an alternative service should be encouraged. The NLA has received government approval and funding to establish an Australian library-based information service. It cannot be established too soon. The initial burst of activity which marked the first two years appears to have expended too much energy, as indicated by a present lull. It is to be hoped that the current inactivity is not due to a loss of direction, but is merely a pause to redeploy forces.

I mentioned earlier that in some instances state libraries tend to behave more like the National Library. This quality is also exemplified by the CSIRO Library and Information Service, which is operating as a national library information network by providing service to the entire country.

W. D. Richardson, former Assistant Director General of the NLA, stated recently: "If the National Library has *a* central role to fill in Australian library services it is one of leadership. The first duty of a leader is to ensure that the necessary resources are available for all to undertake their assigned task."[5] The CSIRO is certainly providing leadership by example. It is to be hoped that the NLA will be able to meet the objectives outlined by Richardson and not fall by the wayside.

It is significant that a number of professional bodies have become increasingly aware of the problems of the information-oriented society. The Royal Australian Chemical Institute and the Institution of Engineers Australia have been influential in pressing for formulation of a national information policy. In March 1975 the Australian Mineral Foundation sponsored the Geoscience Information Seminar which resolved to form an Australian Geoscience Information Association. A working party was elected to pursue the formation of such an association and examine and report on its role. It was instructed to consider the establishment of a coordinating body for geoscience information in relation to any proposed national developments, particularly ALBIS. There was a strong recommendation to create a national geoscience data base and the seminar recommended the immediate extension of the CSIRO's SDI services to cover the geosciences through the use of existing international data bases, ensuring that the Australian material was adequately covered.

It is vital to coordinate all these strands at a national level, not by enforcement of rigid policy, but by recommending standards and by example. The National Library should be able to demonstrate the benefits of new services and alternative methods. More important, it should be able to advise on all aspects of information services, including computing and telecommunications.

There is a scarcity of data available on the information needs and use patterns of research workers and practitioners. There should be further investigation into user needs and existing methods of information gathering both overseas and in Australia. One of the few Australian in-depth studies is that by Maguire and Lovelace of the information needs, usage and attitudes of medical researchers in Australia. This preliminary investigation concluded that, in general: "there is extensive non-use and lack of awareness of information services available to users of medical information; local library services are inadequate at both the community and hospital levels to serve the needs of medical practitioners; and the interlibrary loan network is inadequate, even as it functions in the medical libraries of the larger universities." After evaluating the Australian MEDLARS service, they concluded:

> non-users of MEDLARS appear likely to prefer to use the spoken rather than the written word in disseminating information and to be less literature-oriented than MEDLARS users; MEDLARS could be of use to many who do not use it now, especially to those who feel the lack of a literature alerting service; even among users of MEDLARS there is considerable ignorance of the capabilities and limitations of the system; few MEDLARS users are able to call upon the assistance of a suitable informed librarian to assist them in using this and other information services effectively; a number of MEDLARS users who profess themselves satisfied with the service are not in fact using it to best effect and a number who feel some dissatisfaction do not know that the system could be made to work better for them.[6]

In the Australian environment these findings would apply to any of the data base services being offered, both in government and industry. The CSIRO has been monitoring its service and has come to similar conclusions:

> Not all scientists and technologists are convinced that machine readable techniques are useful. . . . Attitudes can depend upon the field of research, the extent of the literature in the field of interest, and the strength of attachment to traditional methods of acquiring information.
>
> On balance however, the evidence to date in CSIRO indicates that in research there is a significant place for SDI. However to convince scientists of the usefulness of this service, and also achieve optimum benefits, demands good communications between users and information scientists.[7]

Good communications are a basic prerequisite, but much more is required. For example, improvement in library services, particularly inter-library loan and extensive training programs for librarians, is needed. More-over, if we believe these services are vital to the needs of society, we should make society aware of them and provide easy access to them. The concept of the information services librarian was introduced to Australia by F. W. Lancaster in 1974 at the first Special Libraries Section Conference. The knowledge and skill of the information services librarian is urgently needed to overcome the present situation, in which machine-readable reference services are still regarded as something unusual and difficult to access.

No university in the country is currently processing either SDI or retrospective services on a regular production basis. For example, the Univer-sity of Sydney channels requests for MEDLARS, BIOSIS and ERIC to the NLA, and requests for CA CONDENSATES to CSIRO. It is not a question of lack of demand, but rather of finance and expertise to establish and offer these services locally.

RESEARCH AND DEVELOPMENT AND NATIONALISM

The level of government spending on research and development has not allowed significant development of information services. Australian libraries have not been through a period of rich funding such as that which U. S. libraries experienced during the 1960s. Australia spends less per capita on research and development than does Canada, France, Germany, Sweden, the United Kingdom or the United States. The Netherlands, comparable to Australia in population and gross national product, spends about 67 percent more per capita on research and development.[8] However, the last few years have seen a change in government attitude. An awareness of the infor-mation-based society and of the need for a national information policy has developed, and funds have been made available to begin planning.

It has been estimated that Australia produces 2 percent of the world's research; this obviously influences the generation and use of information services. In any country there is a multilevel information requirement to be met. Information in the "hard sciences" disciplines, such as medicine, is valid internationally. On the other hand, the "soft" or social sciences are partisan and relative to the environment; thus, national or international information sources must be supplemented with local information. The integration of these local and international services has affected both hardware and software design and usage.

One of the basic requirements of a national information system is a common retrieval language. Compatibility of all system components would include a common organizational structure, a single information retrieval language, compatible hardware and software, a uniform method of selecting and processing information, and a standard method of documentation and coding. Such compatibility would ensure success, but few national or regional information services have managed to establish it. Institutions seeking to provide effective services would like a uniform processing and searching format. The data base creators are not moved by the same motives. The creation of the machine-readable data base has often been as a by-product or development of the published form; in many cases, as with Index Medicus or ISI, computerization has been undertaken to ecomonize on the production of the printed indexes—that is, to be able to produce them more quickly and to reduce publishing costs. Having achieved this and set up the relevant systems, their answer to suggestions for a uniform, standard processing format is: What's in it for us? On the vexed question of indexing and classification principles, I think it would be extremely difficult to ensure uniformity. Particularly when commercial organizations operate on the principle that success is profit, uniformity will not be achieved. All existing services have already made such a large investment in their products that it is difficult to envisage a change without major government financing. The responsibility lies with the users of these systems; they should state their requirements in an attempt to ensure compatibility in the future.

Australia must be able to create and maintain certain specialized data bases which are endemic to the Australian environment. In addition, there is an obligation to provide people with access to the information they need, which requires operation on a national level or on a regional basis, depending on needs, technology, and certain data bases, e.g., MEDLARS or ERIC. There is also a certain political and economic requirement to develop within the country the skills necessary to run national information systems. In the world context, Australia may well develop as the focal point for Southeast Asia and Oceania and serve as a distribution center.

ALBIS is expected to ascertain the feasibility of the types of services that are required and can be supported in Australia. For example, ALBIS could determine whether it is feasible to establish regional networks in each of the capital cities of the states, or perhaps one or two regional centers serving the east coast. These would be the public sector networks where the NLA or another delegated institution would act as the national or Southeast Asian distribution center. In other instances, users could go directly to commercial entrepreneurs for specialized needs.

COMPUTERS AND TELECOMMUNICATIONS

The other major consideration in setting up machine-readable data bases is that of the current and anticipated advances in computing and telecommunications. It is the telecommunication aspect which I would like to consider here because the local situation again dictates progress. Its development is similar to that of ALBIS—promises and high expectations, but as yet no real solutions.

Since 1960 more than three billion dollars has been spent on building an Australian telecommunications network, and an estimated one percent of the gross national product ($400 million) is being spent annually on further developments.

Today, a centralized information service network can be established by using leased telephone lines, but the practical number of separate stations on one line is limited and· the cost is prohibitive. The basic cost of such a national network can be estimated from the cost of a single leased line from Canberra to each of the other state capitals—$200,000 annually.

The Common User Data Network (CUDN) claimed to provide initially three types of communication—data collection, data distribution and interrogation. Data transmission has been handled via the existing networks, which include telegraph, Telex, telephone and video transmission. These facilities were adequate at first, but the increase in volume of data transmission and the need for high-speed transmission facilities led to the development of a network designed exclusively for digital transmission, the CUDN. The Australian Post Office (APO) has held out the hope of CUDN as the answer to a national information service. CUDN is a system of computer switching centers in each of the capital cities and can support peripherals (VDUs, printers, etc.) throughout Australia.

The advantage of a switched service is that users pay only for the amount of traffic they generate. The APO estimated that costs, based on length of messages sent, would be much lower. For example, an individual message of less than 220 characters would cost about one cent via CUDN. It has also been suggested that international access would be possible as the demand arises.

However, there have been severe problems with CUDN, and it is clear that it cannot meet present demands, let alone those of the future. The problems are both technical and financial and have come to light in the report of the Australian Post Office Commission of Inquiry headed by James Vernon. The original projected installation dates for the multicenter operation of the network were: Brisbane—November 17, 1971; Melbourne—March 13, 1972; Sydney—September 11, 1972; Perth—November 11, 1972; and Adelaide—January 7, 1973. A revised schedule indicated that all centers would be operational in 1974. There have been considerable delays in the installation of the various centers, and none will be connected until September 1977. The Vernon report states that while some delays in completing the facility would have been understandable in view of technical problems likely to arise, a time lag of three years is not reasonable. During negotiations, expansion of the CUDN capacity was decided upon at a cost of $6,200,000, and the APO has closed its customer consulting bureau on CUDN. Because of these problems, there is concern that CUDN will become a captive communications network for a small number of government departments and that its stated aim of providing a public service will not be met. To date it has only two customers.

Telecommunications facilities for economical data transfer by library and information services is therefore not yet a reality in Australia. The facilities offered by telecommunications should be publicized; information centers also need to make their requirements known. It is obvious that there has been insufficient communication to date; STISEC stressed the need to overcome these problems. It is hoped that the recommendations regarding telecommunications will be acted upon.

The development of local data base services has been forced onto the community by the cost of networking. Perhaps the emphasis should be on developing links to the United States for data base services until costs within Australia become feasible. Costs of international communication are decreasing, while internal costs continue to increase.

In the area of computing technology, one of the major difficulties is the unavailability of certain equipment; this is often due to the marketing policy of certain firms, and to the Australian government's policy of protecting local industry. Those attempting to design and install new systems frequently must install obsolete equipment because nothing else is available. Spare parts and maintenance are clearly important considerations in this situation.

I hope that I have been able to convey some of the problems faced by library and information centers in Australia in establishing machine-readable data base services. The major developments to date have been isolated ones in the Australian environment, but there must be some coordination and direction in the future. Plans for an Australian domestic satellite should overcome the present technical and financial problems with hard-wired networks, and the formulation of a national information policy may be considered to be the first step in rationalizing the future development of Australian library and information services.

REFERENCES

1. Australian Bureau of Statistics. *Official Year Book of Australia, No. 59, 1973.* Canberra, Australian Bureau of Statistics, 1974, pp. 136-40.

2. Library Automated Systems Information Exchange. *Survey of Australian Automated Library Systems.* (In process.)

3. Canberra, Australia. National Library. Scientific and Technical Information Services Enquiry Committee. *The STISEC Report; Report to the Council of the National Library of Australia.* Canberra, National Library of Australia, 1973.

4. Australian Bureau of Statistics, *op. cit.,* p. 694.

5. Richardson, W. D. "The National Library of Australia's Role in Co-operative Efforts and Networks," *LASIE* 5:23, Nov./Dec. 1974.

6. Maguire, C., and Lovelace, E. *The Information Needs, Usage and Attitudes of Medical Researchers in Australia; A Preliminary Investigation.* Sydney, School of Librarianship, University of New South Wales, 1974, p. 67.

7. Garrow, C., *et al.* "SDI in CSIRO," *Australian Library Journal* 23:136, May 1974.

8. Australia. Department of Science. *Project Score: Survey and Comparisons of Research Expenditure* (Report No. 5). Canberra, Australian Government Publications, 1973, p. 36.

9. Hams, G. E. "The Importance of Information Services for Development in Telecommunications." Paper presented at a telecommunications seminar, 1973.

Additional References

Bryan, H. *The Library System in the Community.* Paper presented to the International Training Course in the Administration of Library and Information Services, Sydney, 1974.

Cotsell, R. J. L. "Technilib," *LASIE* 4:3-11, May/June 1974.

Grant, N. E. "Data Transmission in the Australian Post Office, *LASIE* 2:15-19, March/April 1972.

Horacek, John. "The VIC Library Network: General Introduction,"*LASIE* 4:14-15, May/June 1974.

Maltby, George F. "LASIE Library Network Seminar: Facilities for Cooperative Efforts and Networks," *LASIE* 5:28-39, Nov./Dec. 1974.

Middleton, M. "INIS: The International Nuclear Information System," *Australian Library Journal* 23:136-40, May 1974.

Peake, Dorothy J. "Library Networks and the Australian Scene: Part II—The Australian Scene," *LASIE* 5:11-17, Nov./Dec. 1974.

Richardson, W. D. "The Role of the National Library in Providing Engineering Information." Paper presented at the Conference on Information for Engineering and Sciences, Sydney, July 18-19, 1974.

Williamson, R. D. "Computer-Based Information Services in APM Ltd.," *Australian Library Journal* 23:141-44+, May 1974.

Appendix

SELECTED LIST OF OPERATIONAL DATA BASES IN AUSTRALIA

Data Base	Institution	Software	Availability
B A Previews	NLA	CAN/SDI	no charge
	CSIRO	in house	not available
C A CONDENSATES	CSIRO	in house	available at cost
COMPENDEX	Dept. of Defence	TEXTPAC	not available
E R I C	NLA	TEXTPAC	no charge
FSTA	CSIRO	in house	available at cost
INIS	AAEC	in house	no charge
INSPEC	CSIRO	in house	available at cost
Institute of Paper Chemistry Abs.	APM	DPS	available at a charge
MARC	NLA	Libramatic Systems	20c per bit
MEDLARS	NLA	NLM	no charge
NTIS	Dept. of Defence	TEXTPAC	not available

BECKY J. LYON
Technical Information Specialist
Lister Hill National Center for Biomedical Communications
National Library of Medicine
Bethesda, Maryland

Mind Transplants, Or The Role Of Computer-Assisted Instruction In The Future Of The Library

The concept of the library has broadened a great deal over the past several years. Since the time of cuneiform tablets in Sumerian civilization, libraries have been concerned with storing and accessing recorded knowledge. For hundreds—even thousands—of years, this recorded knowledge has been in book, manuscript, and picture form, and only within the past ten years have libraries and librarians become increasingly aware of other media as a source of recorded knowledge. More and more progressive schools have integrated these media into a new and bigger creature called the "learning resource center" which has combined the more traditional library functions and services with vehicles less traditional than the printed word.

What does the learning resource center emcompass and why should librarians be concerned with this recently evolved institution? The Carnegie Commission on Higher Education has offered this answer to the question:

> Efforts to free libraries from the restraints of a totally print-oriented mission have been underway for many years. The advent of electronic media and new interest in instructional technology have reinforced this interest. One of the main reasons for changes in attitudes on this subject on the nations's campuses has been a realization that the resources of campus libraries (now frequently called *information centers* or *learning-*

resource centers) have been inadequately utilized in the instructional efforts of colleges and universities. A manifestation of the new attitude is the physical location of the library at the core of the main instructional facility on several new, small campuses.

A long-standing objection of tradition-bound librarians to the new roles for information centers was breached in 1969 when a joint Committee of the American Association of School Librarians and the Department of Audio Visual Instruction of the National Education Association (now the Association for Educational Communications and Technology) issued a report strongly recommending unification of print and nonprint media in "media centers." As one writer said of the report, "... the *Standards* recommends a unified media program in which a single institution within the school provides all necessary materials for learning; and quantitatively it prescribes ways for achieving this objective. The words 'library,' 'librarian,' 'audiovisual center' and 'audiovisual specialist' are entirely supplanted by terms such as 'media center' and 'media specialist.' The media center will house *all* learning materials and accompanying services, putting audiovisual and printed resources under an allegedly more favorable single administrative organization and providing easier access for individual or group study.[1]

The handling of instructional media creates a totally new set of problems for the librarian who must become familiar with a new group of materials which often require modifications of existing routines and policies. These affect all areas, including cataloging, classification, storage, retrieval and circulation. In addition, these modalities require specialized equipment, which evokes a myriad of nightmares associated with the procurement, care and feeding of this equipment.

Assuming that this does not paint a rosy picture, the handling of media must be approached from a positive perspective. Other areas in librarianship present equally challenging facets—who among us has not struggled with the Anglo-American cataloging rules? Media and instructional technology are here to stay, according to the Carnegie Commission and educators of all types. In the medical field, for instance, the Association of American Medical Colleges reports that of 135 medical schools in the United States and Canada, 101 have an established unit responsible for instructional materials development and/or management of media.

The implications of this new technology are: (1) the library will become a more dominant feature of the campus, (2) students will need more familiarity with computers as they enter college, and (3) faculty will need to be trained in the use of new technologies.

Up to this point, I have not considered any specific type of media; now I shall reveal my purposes for this lengthy preamble. The learning resource center of the present is primarily concerned with films, videotapes, cassettes, filmstrips, sound recordings, and many other audiovisual modalities. However, there is an important format on the horizon which many libraries have not yet explored: computer-assisted instruction (CAI).

CAI may well represent the next phase in the involvement of the library or learning resource center in the educational process. I will begin to explain this statement by describing the Lister Hill Center and our experience with CAI.

The Lister Hill National Center for Biomedical Communications had its start in 1965, when the Committee on Appropriations of the House of Representatives encouraged the National Library of Medicine to develop a research capability. On August 3, 1968, President Johnson signed Public Law 90-456, which authorized the creation of the center. Soon after the center's establishment, Martin Cummings, Director of the National Library of Medicine (NLM), asked the Association of American Medical Colleges (AAMC) to take a leadership position in involving the academic medical community in planning a biomedical communications network. A conference was held in February 1969 to consider the educational services that a network might provide.[2] Subsequently, a request for more specific plans resulted in the production of a report from the steering committee of the Council of Academic Societies, Association of American Medical Colleges.[3] The steering committee report included many recommendations, one of which states: "The Steering Committee advocates the organization of a biomedical communications network designed to meet some of the needs of medical education and medical practice and to capitalize on the current state of development of various phases of communications and computer technology. Of primary importance is the requirement to maintain a high level of learning experiences for growing numbers of students to whom medical, dental, nursing and other health career schools are committed."[4]

The AAMC report was presented to the Board of Regents of NLM and the board appointed a Priorities Review Committee to study the report. The committee presented four recommendations which were adopted unanimously by the regents. One of these recommendations has a direct bearing on the establishment of the Experimental CAI Network. It read: "The Committee advocates the organization of a biomedical communications network fundamentally conceived as providing the mechanism by means of which interinstitutional sharing of resources will be used to meet some of the needs of medical education."[5] Implementation of this goal began in September 1971.

In response to this recommendation, the Lister Hill Center Experimental CAI Network was established in July 1972 to test the feasibility of sharing CAI materials through a national computer network. Three suppliers of CAI programs and one commercial time-sharing corporation were under contract to the library to realize the network concept collectively. The three centers of CAI expertise were the Ohio State University (OSU), the Massachusetts

General Hospital (MGH) and the University of Illinois Medical Center (UIMC) in Chicago. In January 1974, a decision to focus University of Illinois support on the PLATO (Programmed Logic for Automatic Teaching Operation) project necessitated UIMC's withdrawal from the network; since that time we have been operating with the two remaining systems. The Illinois CASE (Computer Aided Simulation of the Clinical Encounter) programs were subsequently transferred to the Ohio State computer.

The network configuration itself allows the OSU and MGH computers to be connected to the TYMSHARE network via minicomputers so that the user need only call one location (i.e., the nearest network node) to be linked to either computer by telephone line. For many users this does not even involve a long distance telephone charge. This network also allows the programs to remain on the host computers so that maintenance and update responsibility reside with the program supplier.

There are programs on the network applicable to health science users in medicine, dentistry, nursing, pharmacology, and allied health professions at all levels—undergraduate, graduate and continuing education. Available programs include microbiology, genetics, biochemistry, physiology and anatomy in basic sciences; cardiopulmonary resuscitation, abdominal pain, diabetic ketoacidosis and coma in clinical simulations; and several natural-language interactive patient encounters in various specialty areas. These programs have been used in a variety of ways by more than 100 health science institutions using 1500-3000 hours of program time per month.

Network Costs

Costs are divided into three main categories: TYMSHARE costs, contractor costs, and NLM staff costs. The TYMSHARE cost is subdivided into fixed costs and costs which vary with increased usage. The fixed costs include the rental of the interface minicomputers at each site, maintenance of the user name file, cost per log-in, and invoice preparation. The variable portion of the TYMSHARE cost is broken down into connect time and characters transmitted. The contractor costs are divided into two parts: the charge for the computer costs, and the charge for personnel support. Table 1 shows the total CAI cost per terminal hour, assuming 1800 terminal hours usage per month.

Initially, the network was free to users. It was later decided to have network users pay an increasing portion of the cost. In February 1974 the charge was $2.50 per hour and in July 1974 it was raised to $5.00 per connect hour.

Although user charges had initially caused a drop in the number of institutions who had access to the programs, that number has now risen to a

Component	Cost (per terminal hour)[b]
TYMSHARE variable communication cost	$ 5.43
TYMSHARE fixed communication cost	
(TYCOMS, user names, invoice preparation)	3.28
Computer port charges	4.66
Computer host personnel support costs	4.69
NLM Central Staff	1.66
Total	$19.72

[a] Does not include user institution costs for terminals, personnel, materials, or local communications facilities.

[b] Terminal hours are not always the same as student instruction hours. Students may work together in small groups.

Table 1. CAI Costs Per Terminal Hour[a]

Source: Rubin, Martin L., *et al. Evaluation of the Experimental CAI Network (1973-1975) of the Lister Hill National Center for Biomedical Communications, National Library of Medicine.* Alexandria, Va., National Technical Information Service, 1975.

peak of more than seventy-five users. The number of hours used also dropped, but has been slowly increasing over the past few months (see Figure 1). The interest that has been generated in the network is evidenced by the evolution of an active user group. Largely due to the fact that the library announced more than one year ago that it would not fund the network after May 31, 1975, users formed the Health Education Network Users Group (HENUG) to investigate means of making the programs available after May 31. This group has negotiated with OSU, MGH and TYMSHARE and produced plans for what it hopes will be a viable continuation. For an $8.00-$10.00 per hour charge, users will be able to access the CAI programs through TYMSHARE for a period of ten additional months. During this time, HENUG plans to explore alternatives to the present configuration in the hope of decreasing hourly rates.

The experimental network and user group are unique to networking and to the field of computer-assisted instruction. The network was the first national attempt to make CAI available across institutional lines, and it brought this form of instructional material to the attention of many persons who otherwise would not have had the opportunity to examine programs and student reactions to the programs on a local level. The user group is unique in that it is the first group to attempt networking on a self-supporting basis. At present we have no real indication of the success or failure of this effort, but it is an important step toward the interinstitutional sharing of resources.

Figure 1. Number of Hours Used, April 1973-February 1975

The conclusion reached by many as a result of the experiment is that CAI in the health sciences is in its infancy, but that it is a viable teaching/learning modality. However, in the early stages of the network, we were not acute in our perception of where CAI should be marketed. At the insistence of the contractors, we deliberately aimed at the departmental faculty by establishing a dichotomy between "operational" and "trial" users, and by insisting that the "operational users" submit an "Educational Material Use and Evaluation Plan," promise to strive to integrate our course offerings into their curricula, and even train their faculty to produce additional units of instruction. We did not, perhaps because it would have been too easy, circularize our MEDLINE users. We were polite to those few librarians who did manage to find out that the network existed, but gently indicated that they could not possibly muster the faculty involvement required to do all the good things that we wanted. (One such librarian put the quietus to that argument by returning the next week with his dean in tow, and said, "Would you mind repeating that part where I can't get faculty involvement?")

Location	Number
Libraries and learning resource centers	48
Medical school departments	23
Computer laboratories	18
Terminal rooms	5
Student study areas, residents lounges	5
Conference rooms	4
Offices of medical education	4
Physicians' offices	4
Emergency rooms	3
Ward rooms	2
Cardiac care units	2

Table 2. Location of CAI Terminals on LHC Experiment

Institution	Terminal Location
University of California-Los Angeles	Library
University of Pennsylvania	Library
Harvard Medical School	Library
Medical College of Virginia	Library
University of Washington	Learning Resource Center
University of Texas-San Antonio	Library
Stanford University	Learning Resource Center
University of Arizona	Library
George Washington University	Library
University of Oregon	Computer Center and Educational Resources Facility

Table 3. Location of Terminals with Highest Mean Usage

Despite this shunning of libraries, we found that a large number of the terminals on our network—even some of our major users—were in fact in libraries. Table 2 shows a location breakdown of terminals used for CAI, and Table 3 shows that of the ten largest users, nine were centers managed by libraries or learning resource centers.

Given that instructional technology, and more specifically computer-assisted instruction, is here to stay, how can librarians use it to their advantage? The network concept has demonstrated that schools are willing to share CAI materials; however, the present configuration is too costly for the long run. Therefore, alternative distribution methods must be explored. We are looking at computer language translation to allow wider distribution of existing and future materials, which would spread developmental costs more evenly. We are also examining the use of minicomputers at the institutional level for providing programs to on-site users.

The minicomputer has advantages for both the library and the development of CAI. It allows the creation and maintenance of CAI programs at an individual institution, alleviating problems of tailoring imported materials to fit a curriculum. In addition, a minicomputer is a far less expensive piece of computer equipment to procure than a monstrous central computer. Its use lowers communications costs which can be prohibitive to the user in Boise, Idaho, whose nearest network node is in Denver.

For the library, a minicomputer can be the answer to problems in library automation. Strides are being made toward its use in library systems, which offers many benefits also found in CAI. At the University of Minnesota Bio-medical Library, Glenn Brudvig and his staff are designing a total library system supported by a minicomputer and funded through a grant from NLM's Extramural Programs Division. A brief survey of automation projects, however, reveals that few libraries have discovered the virtues of minicomputers. A local minicomputer is less expensive to obtain and operate than a larger configuration. In addition, the larger computer is nearly always shared with other parts of the institution and library functions are frequently of low priority. This means that systems must be designed to run in batch mode (to be updated during nonprime hours), and often the librarian does not have access to the file during regular working hours. The combined needs of a CAI system and automation project in the library could conceivably justify the procurement of a minicomputer for use by the library or learning resource center.

Another alternative to large network CAI also has implications for the library. We are currently exploring the use of "intelligent terminals" for the purpose of supplying CAI. An intelligent terminal is simply a desk-top device with keyboard display and a small memory, which is entirely self-contained. By plugging in the terminal and loading the CAI program by cassette tape, an entire program library can be made easily available. This device lends itself particularly well to use in the library because it requires little technical knowledge, no programming support, and does not depend on the up-down time of a larger computer.

The writing of new programs is also simplified by an authoring language which has been tailored specifically to the intelligent terminal. PILOT, as the language is named, can eliminate the authoring stumbling block by encouraging faculty to attempt creation of their own programs. Prior to this development, most authoring has been done in conjunction with programmers because of the technical level of the authoring language. This has discouraged many faculty members who have neither the time nor inclination to spend with a more cumbersome process.

A few years ago, a colleague of mine was approached by a salesman for a commercial abstract service. He raised an eyebrow at the price—over $1000 per year—and asked what luck the salesman had in selling his service to libraries. He answered, "I don't sell it to libraries—it's too expensive for them. I sell it to directors of research, who keep it in their offices."

Computer-assisted instruction has had similar problems over the years. Academic departments, computer science laboratories, and specialists in instructional technology have combined forces to develop these programs. The pathways from computer to user have all too often bypassed the library. Librarians may well have been aware of these programs, but never thought of them as coming within their scope.

We think that libraries will find computer-assisted instruction a useful service to offer their clientele. However, it is wise to keep in mind the fact that CAI is different from other library and audiovisual materials. CAI is a living, dynamic tool which actively involves the user, we think that this makes it an even more desirable addition to the library. David Kronick, librarian at the University of Texas Health Center, San Antonio, said, "Anyone who sits at a terminal interacting with a computer based teaching program must feel the presence of another fine and active intelligence who is using the computer as an effective intermediary and thus providing greater access to his teaching skills."[5]

The fact that CAI lives is evidenced by comments received from students themselves: "It was very useful to help develop clinical judgments"; "This program was realistic, stimulating, and a good review of a topic which many internists lose familiarity with soon after leaving their residency and fellowship years"; and "Although I realize that the computer is expensive, I feel that its use by students is extremely beneficial."

Although computer-assisted instruction is still in the experimental stages, its potential as a learning resource is becoming more and more apparent. However, I hope that every learning resource center of the future—no matter how many minicomputers, intelligent terminals, videotape projectors and biofeedback sensory learning carrels—will still maintain a stock of books.

REFERENCES

1. Carnegie Commission on Higher Education. *The Fourth Revolution: Instructional Technology in Higher Education*. Berkeley, Calif., McGraw-Hill, 1972, p. 33.

2. Smythe, Cheves McC. *Potential Education Services from a National Biomedical Communications Network*. Washington, D. C., Association of American Medical Colleges, 1969.

3. Stead, Eugene A., Jr., *et al.*, eds. "Educational Technology for Medicine: Roles for the Lister Hill Center," *Journal of Medical Education* 46(7, part 2):1-97, July 1971.

4. *Ibid.*, p. 83.

5. Priorities Review Committee. Recommendations to the Board of Regents. Oct. 14, 1971, p. 3. (Unpublished)

6. Kronick, David A., *et al. Remote Access Computer Assisted Instruction: A User's Guide and Catalog.* San Antonio, University of Texas, 1974, p. 4.

Additional References

Wooster, Harold. "The Lister Hill Experimental CAI Network—A Progress Report," *The Physiologist* 16:626-30, Nov. 1973.

Wooster, Harold, and Lewis, Jinnet F. "Distribution of Computer-Assisted Instructional Materials in Biomedicine through the Lister Hill Center Experimental Network," *Computers in Biology and Medicine* 3:319-23, Oct. 1973.

──────. "The Utility of Computer Assisted Instruction—An Experimental Network. In *Information Utilities: Proceedings of the 37th ASIS Annual Meeting.* Vol. 11. Washington, D. C., American Society for Information Science, 1974.

DAVID L. WALTZ
Assistant Professor of Electrical Engineering
and Research Assistant Professor
Coordinated Science Laboratory
University of Illinois
Urbana-Champaign, Illinois

Natural-Language
Question-Answering Systems

In his excellent book, *Libraries of the Future*,[1] J.C.R. Licklider paints an elaborate picture of what libraries may become by the year 2000. He sees libraries as being accessible through and augmented by digital computer programs and evolving into "procognitive systems," or general aids to thinking. Many library documents, as well as much text, such as that of computer-typeset books have already been made computer-readable. But how far have we come in devising programs that do this reading automatically? And how close are we to systems that can understand users' questions, comments and commands? These are questions I will attempt to answer in this paper.

The systems I will describe all deal primarily with facts rather than documents. I assume that facts are inherently more difficult to deal with, and that documents are a special case of fact.

Since there is a limited amount of space for this presentation, and I wish to put forth some idea of what can be done with current natural-language question-answering systems, I will concentrate on the behavior of the

This work is supported in part by the Office of Naval Research under Contract N00014-67-A-0305 and in part by Joint Services Electronics Program (U. S. Army, U. S. Navy and U. S. Air Force) under Contract DAAB-07-72-C-0259.

systems, and not go into as much detail about how the systems work. I will, however, leave adequate pointers so that those who wish to find more information can do so.

A Brief History

Natural-language technology has advanced dramatically in the last fifteen years. We now have some systems which are not toys, but are in active use by researchers; furthermore, we have a much better idea of what is necessary to generate programs more capable of understanding language in the next generation.

To get an idea of the size of this change, let us first consider BASE-BALL, one of the earliest natural-language systems.[2] BASEBALL, written in 1961, answered questions about baseball data comparing month, day, place, teams and scores for each game in the American League for one year. In this limited context, a very small vocabulary was sufficient, since relatively few types of questions could be asked. Furthermore, a user's language was severely constrained. Sentences could contain no dependent clauses, no logical connectives like *and, or,* and *not*), no constructions with relations like *highest* and *most,* and no reference to sequential facts, as in: Did the Red Sox ever win six games *in a row?* Examples of questions BASEBALL could answer include: Who did the Red Sox lose to on July 5? Did every team play at least once in each park in each season? What teams won ten games in July?

BASEBALL operated by parsing its questions, and then transforming the parsed question into a standard "specification list." The question-answering routine took this canonical form as the meaning of the question. Thus "Who did the Red Sox lose to on July 5?" was transformed into the specification list:

```
Team (losing)    = Boston
Date             = July 5
Team (winning)   = ?
```

Aside from its grammatical limitations within its domain of expertise, BASEBALL had the following limitations:

1. It could be extended to new domains only by extensive reprogramming.
2. It either understood a sentence fully, or did not understand it at all—no provision was made for saving understood portions of sentences or for interacting with the user to ask clarifying questions.
3. It could not understand pronoun reference.
4. It had no ability to accept declarative information; for example, it was

not possible to add to its data base by telling it "The Red Sox beat the Yankees on July 10."

5. A user could not add procedural information, e.g., one could not add to its linguistic ability, nor give it advice in any form.

6. Because its universe of discourse was so limited, BASEBALL's writers simply never had to worry about handling ambiguous requests.

In contrast, there exist today programs which exhibit—at least to some degree—all abilities mentioned above that BASEBALL lacked. I will briefly describe three programs—those of Woods, Winograd, and Schank—and will then discuss some ideas (principally those of Minsky) which suggest methods for writing vastly more powerful language-understanding programs.

LUNAR

The LUNAR system developed by Woods[3] answers questions about a fairly large data base of samples of lunar rocks and soils. While the data base, like BASEBALL's data base, contains only a small number of data types, the LUNAR system is much more flexible than BASEBALL, most dramatically in its linguistic ability. It is able to accept grammatically complex sentences involving nested dependent clauses, comparative and superlative adjective forms, and some types of anaphoric reference. For example, Woods's system is capable of answering all of the following questions: What is the average concentration of aluminum in high alkalai rocks? Has the mineral analcite been identified in any lunar samples? What are those samples? Give me all model analyses of lunar fines. List the rocks which contain chromite and ulvospinel. What minerals have been identified in lunar samples? What is the concentration of lanthanum in rock S10034? The system was demonstrated at a geology conference only six months after work had begun on the project; the system was then able to answer 78 percent of the questions solicited from the audience. It was judged that the system would have been able to answer 90 percent if the program code had been perfected.

Woods's system uses an augmented transition network (ATN) to parse sentences, and then generates a formal query by patching together the code fragments which represent each phrase in the sentence. Like BASEBALL, then, it attempts to produce something like a specifications list, except that it has a much larger set of lists to choose from and is more clever about concatenating them.

I mention Woods's system especially because his work seems most easily extendable to new domains. In fact, it seems to be quite neatly extendable to document retrieval systems; however, extending it to understand text would definitely be a major task.

SHRDLU

SHRDLU, a natural-language system written by Terry Winograd[4] operates in an environment called the "blocks world." SHRDLU is given an internal description of a scene made up of blocks of different shapes (cubes, bricks, pyramids, etc.) plus a box on a table. The system has a single robot hand under its control, which can pick up one block at a time. A user can give the robot commands to move blocks around (e.g., "pick up a big red block"), ask questions about the scene ("Are there any blue blocks in the box?"), about the robot's actions ("Why did you pick up the green block?"), or give SHRDLU procedural information through declarative sentences ("A steeple is a stack containing two green cubes and a pyramid").

SHRDLU keeps a record of its own goals and subgoals. The following is a typical dialog, assuming that SHRDLU has earlier been told to pick up the red block:

User: Why did you pick up the green block?
SHRDLU: To get rid of it.
User: Why did you do that?
SHRDLU: So I could pick up the red block.
User: Why did you do that?
SHRDLU: Because you asked me to.

Furthermore, the system records declarative information in a form that allows it to use the information either to answer questions or to carry out instructions. Thus, after being told what a steeple is, a user may ask "Are there any steeples on the table now?" which SHRDLU will answer appropriately, using the procedural information to check for an instance of a steeple in the data base. Alternatively, the user may say, "Build a steeple," in which case SHRDLU will do so, using the definition of a steeple to construct a program to carry out the building of the structure.

SHRDLU can carry out a dialog with a user to clairfy sentences. For example, if asked, "Are there any purple pyramids on the red block?" it may in turn ask the user, "Do you mean directly on top of, or supported by?"—unless the answer in both cases is "no."

Finally, as illustrated throughout this section, SHRDLU can handle pronoun and phrase reference (e.g., "Why did you do *that*?"), and it can accept arbitrarily complicated sentence structures (e.g., "Does the shortest thing the tallest pyramid's support supports support anything green?").

SHRDLU does this by interpreting all sentences as procedures (i.e., programs) which are then executed to search its data base, or to run block manipulation programs, or to generate new programs. It uses MICROPLAN-NER,[5] a programming language designed especially to simplify finding items which satisfy a goal, like GOAL (?X IN BOX), either by searching the data base for an item ?X which is in the box (pattern-directed data base search), or by calling programs which will change the scene and data base so that there is some item ?X in the box (pattern-directed procedure invocation). MICRO-PLANNER also contains facilities for automatic backup, so that variables can be assigned tentative values which can later be taken back if they do not work out. Thus, the MICROPLANNER program

```
(GOAL (?X IN BOX))
(GOAL (?X IS-A BLOCK))
(GOAL (COLOR ?X YELLOW))
(GOAL (SUPPORTS ?X ?Y))
(GOAL (?Y IS-A PYRAMID))
   (PICK-UP ?X)
```

represents the English sentence, "Pick up any yellow block in the box which supports a pyramid"; the program will automatically try various values for ?X and ?Y until it either succeeds in satisfying all the goals, or until it has exhausted all possible choices for ?X and ?Y.

Winograd's program was modified to answer questions about weather data, but there are difficulties in extending it. First, either the data base on which SHRDLU operates must be rewritten in a MICROPLANNER form (single-level list structures only), or the outive system would have to be extensively reprogrammed. Thus, it seems unreasonable to use the program on a data base such as one of English text. Secondly, the system seems to support naturally only a single context of discourse. While the data base can obviously be made to include items from any number of contexts, MICRO-PLANNER has no way of neatly segmenting the data base into coherent pieces. Thus, large-scale data bases cannot be easily supported.

MARGIE

MARGIE[6] (Memory Analysis, Response Generation and Inference on English), developed by Schank, is not a question-answering system, but does shed considerable light on the issues important in automatic text understanding. MARGIE accepts sentences about a wide range of topics and stores them in a semantic-net-like structure called a "conceptual dependency diagram." Conceptual dependency diagrams are intended to be canonical deep structures of the input sentences. These diagrams can then be used to generate inferences from or paraphrases of the input sentence.

If MARGIE is told in its inference mode that "John gave Mary an aspirin," it will produce the following output:

John believes that Mary wants an aspirin.
Mary is sick.
Mary wants to feel better.
Mary will ingest the aspirin.
etc.

If given "John killed Mary by choking Mary," the system in paraphrase mode will produce:

John strangled Mary.
John choked Mary and she died because she could not breathe.
Mary died because she was unable to inhale some air and she was unable to
    inhale some air because John grabbed her neck.

Conceptual dependency diagrams are formed by replacing all verbs with structures involving twelve basic "ACTS"; Schank argues that these are sufficient to express any verb meaning. The ACTS are: CONC (conceptualize), MTRANS (transfer mental item), ATRANS (transfer possession of article), PTRANS (change location of object), MOVE (body parts), PROPEL (apply a force to), GRASP, INGEST, EXPEL, ATTEND (direct sense organ at something), MBUILD (add information to memory) and SPEAK.

"John grew corn with fertilizer" is represented by the following conceptual dependency diagram:

This can be read as "John caused corn to increase in size by transferring fertilizer from somewhere to the ground around the corn." Thus it can be seen that a substantial amount of structure is attached to the word *grow*. This structure represents the relationships that obtain between the other words in the sentence, using the various symbols in the diagram, each of which has precise meanings.

The structure has slots for other words: *grow* in this case has slots for an agent (John), a plant (corn), an object (fertilizer), as well as slots for instruments (e.g., hoe), which are not filled in this case. Each slot has associated with it semantic markers which select the types of phrases or words appropriate for the slot. The words which appear in the sentence can be checked against the slots in the verb structure to select the appropriate meaning of the verb. Thus the meaning of *grow* in "John grew the corn" requires a human agent and plant object, whereas the meanings of *grow* in "John grew" or "the corn grew" or "John grew pigs" or "John grew warts" require different types of slot-filling elements. MARGIE uses this slot-filling technique to avoid parsing the sentence in any traditional sense.

Each structure also has links to plausible inferences which can be drawn from the sentences. The system can infer from "John grew the corn" that "John will probably harvest the corn," "John probably wants to either sell the corn or eat the·corn," and so on. In a full text-understanding system, these inferences could be used to answer questions not explicitly contained in the text, or to verify the accuracy of its interpretations by comparing the text following a sentence with what the system judges to be appropriate follow-up statements. The system could also be made to understand that a statement such as "John grew the corn and then threw it away" is unusual and requires some additional explanation.

Frame Theory

Minsky has recently written a paper concerning the theory of *frames*, which are semantic structures reminiscent of conceptual dependency diagrams.[7] Like the diagrams, frames have relations, slots, default values and semantic markers, but unlike them, frames may also contain procedural information, and need not correspond only to verbs. Frame theory argues that statements such as "John is a doctor" actually express a complex of plausible inferences simultaneously: John is a physician, John probably has knowledge of anatomy and medication, John may have a specialty, John probably likes to play golf, etc.

Minsky's key idea is that language does not involve the transfer of structures from one speaker to another, as much as it does the selection of a structure in the hearer, and an instantiation of some values in this structure. In this view, listening is an active process, and inherently involves projection (in the psychological sense) on the part of the listener. For example, many jokes are "funny" because the unexpected happens. In any given communication, a number of frames are selected, including a frame for the type of communication (lecture, argument, story, chat, etc.), as well as a frame for topics.

In a large-scale text-understanding and question-answering system, one can imagine frames being selected by the use of keywords, and being verified by matching; this system allows effective segmentation of a system's knowledge into contexts, but also provides links between various contexts. Problems of ambiguity can often be avoided by knowing the context of the communication; "The group lacked an identity" is only ambiguous if we do not know whether the discourse context is mathematics or psychology. Speed and efficiency can be greatly improved by keeping only the current context in primary storage.

Finally, depth of understanding can be greatly increased through the application of frame theory ideas. Anaolgy and metaphor can be understood as frame transfers; even some poetry and humor may be understandable.[8]

There is every reason to believe that the next generation of language-understanding systems will be as dramatic an improvement over current systems as current systems have been over those of fifteen years ago. While none of the systems described here deals explicitly with current library problems, the descendants of these systems could eventually revolutionize the entire structure of libraries, as well as the lives of all those who use and benefit from libraries.

REFERENCES

1. Licklider, J. C. R. *Libraries of the Future.* Cambridge, Mass., M. I. T. Press, 1965.

2. Green, Bert F., Jr., *et al.* "BASEBALL: An Automatic Question Answerer." *In* Edward A. Feigenbaum and Julian Feldman, eds. *Computers and Thought.* New York, McGraw-Hill, 1963, pp. 207-16.

3. Woods, W. A., *et al.* "The Lunar Sciences Natural Language Information System: Final Report" (BBN Report No. 2378). Cambridge, Mass., Bolt, Beranek and Newman, 1972.

4. Winograd, Terry. *Understanding Natural Language.* New York, Academic Press, 1972.

5. Sussman, G. J., *et al.* "MICRO-PLANNER Reference Manual" (Memo No. 203A). Cambridge, Mass., M. I. T. Artificial Intelligence Lab, 1971.

6. Schank, Roger, *et al.* "MARGIE: Memory, Analysis, Response Generation, and Inference on English." In *Advanced Papers of the Third International Joint Conference on Artificial Intelligence.* Stanford, Calif., Stanford University, 1973, pp. 255-61; and Schank, Roger C. "Identification of Conceptualizations Underlying Natural Language." *In* Roger C. Schank and Kenneth M. Colby, eds. *Computer Models of Thought and Language.* San Francisco, W. H. Freeman; 1973, pp. 187-247.

7. Minsky, Marvin L. "A Framework for Representing Knowledge" (Memo No. 306). Cambridge, Mass., M. I. T. Artificial Intelligence Lab, 1974.

8. Waltz, David L. "On Understanding Poetry." Paper presented at a Conference on Theoretical Issues in Natural Language Processing, June 10-13, 1975, M. I. T., Cambridge, Mass.

F. WILFRID LANCASTER
Professor
Graduate School of Library Science
University of Illinois
Urbana-Champaign, Illinois

Have Information Services Been Successful? A Critique

This paper is somewhat different from those presented earlier. The others have dealt with experiences in the provision of information services through the use of machine-readable data bases. By and large, they reported successes. The present paper is more a series of observations and impressions on the achievements of the field of information service in the past twenty years. In particular, it is my intention: (1) to point out certain failures, or at least limitations, of existing information services, (2) to mention some findings on use and users of information services that seem to be of special significance, and (3) to suggest some directions for future work. I intend here to raise questions rather than to answer them. In parts, at least, the paper is deliberately provocative and should be viewed in this light.

> An information retrieval system will tend *not* to be used whenever it is more painful and troublesome for a customer to have information than for him not to have it.

This statement was made in 1960 by Calvin Mooers[1] and is frequently referred to as "Mooers's Law." It is perhaps the single most important quotation in the entire literature on the provision of information service.

Convenience appears to be the single most important factor determining whether or not an information service will be used. It is the overriding consideration in the information-seeking behavior of professional people. It has been shown by a number of investigators, most notably by Allen and Gerstberger[2] and by Rosenberg,[3] that professionals needing information are likely to turn first to the most convenient source, even if they recognize that another source is in some sense better (e.g., more complete or more current). In studies of information-seeking behavior in various subject fields, when professionals are asked to rank information sources in order of importance, libraries consistently appear rather low in the rankings. In fact, formal information sources in general may be ranked rather low. A number of these studies have revealed that personal files are extremely important sources of information and that these files are likely to be the first source that a professional will turn to when the need for information arises. Soper discovered that there is a strong tendency for a bibliographic item cited by an author to appear in his personal collection, and that this tendency applies to the humanities and social sciences as well as to the field of science.[4]

If the personal files do not provide the information needed, the professional is quite likely to turn to an informal channel of communication. He or she will contact a professional colleague, in the same institution or outisde it, frequently by telephone. It has long been recognized that in virtually all fields there exist well developed networks of informal communication, sometimes referred to as "invisible colleges." If a sociometric analysis is applied to a community of information users, it is likely to reveal a number of sociometric stars or information gatekeepers—individuals to whom others turn for information. An elaborate and effective communication network is built around these stars, and information flow within such a network has been referred to in epidemiological terms. Crawford, among others, has pointed out that information supplied to the sociometric stars is likely to spread through the community like an infection.[5] This seems to be a phenomenon highly significant for the design and implementation of information services.

I recently completed a study that highlights in several ways the importance that convenience plays in the acquisition of information.[6] The study relates to information-seeking behavior in the neurosciences. The recipients of two current awareness publications of a specialist nature (one relating to Parkinson's disease and one to brain chemistry) were asked to rank information sources in order of their importance. The single most important source, even in these highly specialized areas, was *Current Contents*, a general alerting mechanism. There seem to be a number of good reasons for the importance of this publication, including its convenient format and the fact that it is a very current information source (at least as far as the journal literature goes). There is another extremely important reason: the publication provides convenient sources for document delivery, both by its guaranteed tearsheet service and by the fact that it supplies addresses of authors to facilitate the requesting of reprints. Of the several hundred neuroscientists who participated in this study, the great majority seem to favor a document source that they can use without leaving their desks (through a postcard requesting a reprint or a tearsheet) rather than a source that usually requires a personal visit (an academic or special library) and the use of procedures that may sometimes seem bureaucratic. It seems clear that in building their own document collections many scientists rely rather heavily on writing to other scientists for reprints of their articles, another manifestation of informal channels of communication. It is interesting to note that, in this study, the inclusion or exclusion of the addresses of authors was regarded as a highly significant factor in the evaluation of printed current awareness devices. Once more, ease of use and personal convenience are shown to be factors of paramount importance in the evaluation of an information source. I will return to this later.

The Achievements of Information Services

There is little doubt that giant strides have been made in the provision of information service in the past twenty years. The application of computers to information retrieval has allowed a depth of indexing, and a depth and complexity of search, that was virtually impossible in earlier systems. The application of computers to the printing and publishing industries has led to the generation of numerous machine-readable data bases that can, in turn, be used to provide other forms of information service, both current and retrospective. Computer-based selective dissemination of information (SDI) to individuals or to groups offers a more efficient, comprehensive current awareness service than any provided earlier. The computer has also been used to generate new printed tools, including citation indexes, which would be almost impossible to construct on a large scale by purely manual processes, and specialized bibliographies produced essentially as by-products of more comprehensive publications (e.g., the recurring bibliographies of the National Library of Medicine). The computer has also permitted us to obtain a reasonable level of access to the previously elusive report literature through publication and retrieval systems developed by the National Technical Information Service (NTIS), the Defense Documentation Center (DDC), the Educational Resources Information Center (ERIC), the International Nuclear Information System (INIS), and others.

Automation has considerably extended the possibilities for cooperation among libraries and information centers. Machine-readable files can be shipped around rather easily so that truly national and international services can be developed. The paper by Dagmar Schmidmaier, elsewhere in this volume, gives an example of how one country (in this case Australia) may build information services around data bases created in other countries.

The availability of MARC tapes from the Library of Congress has greatly increased the possibilities for shared cataloging, perhaps best exemplified by the operations of the Ohio College Library Center. We can now see the beginnings of several important union catalogs and lists of serial holdings in on-line form.

It is likely that we will see more cooperative schemes whereby a number of libraries will share a central computer facility accessed by means of on-line terminals located throughout the member institutions for a wide range of bibliographic activities including acquisitions, cataloging, serials control, circulation control and interlibrary lending. Through an on-line network the files of all libraries in such a group, including their catalogs, can be physically far removed from the libraries themselves, yet readily accessible.

Another emerging important form of cooperation is the regional information center, as exemplified by the Northeast Academic Science Information Center (NASIC), described elsewhere in this volume by Wax. The goal of such a center is to provide access to a wide range of machine-readable files from a whole group of libraries in a designated geographic region.

Without much doubt, the greatest single development of the last decade in the provision of information service has been the move to on-line retrieval capabilities. On-line systems for information retrieval have all of the capabilities of off-line systems without any of their major disadvantages. On-line systems provide relatively immediate results, are interactive and heuristic (avoiding the blind one-shot searches that are characteristic of off-line systems), and allow various forms of browsing. On-line systems have *greatly* extended our capacity for machine literature searching by greatly increasing the number of centers with computer searching capabilities, and greatly enlarging the universe of librarians competent and experienced in this aspect of reference service. In certain types of libraries—particularly medical, industrial, and governmental—on-line terminals are now being used quite routinely in the provision of reference service. In these libraries, use of the on-line terminal is integrated with use of the more traditional information sources in printed form. In the papers in this volume by Dowlin and by Summit and Drew, we learn of two forms of exploitation of machine-readable files by public libraries. The extension of computer-based reference services to public libraries is truly an exciting development.

As a result of all of these activities, a new type of librarian is emerging: the information services librarian is a professional who specializes in the provision of information service from machine-readable data bases. As described elsewhere,[7] the information services librarian needs knowledge and skills beyond those normally found in a more "conventional" librarian. The information services librarian needs to know what exists in the way of machine-readable files, where these files are located, and how to obtain service from them. This librarian may also be required to evaluate both data bases and service centers, and therefore needs to know something of evaluation methodology. In order to exploit machine-readable files effectively, the information services librarian needs to know a considerable amount about indexing techniques and about vocabulary control procedures, as well as about searching strategy. Clearly, the emergence of the information services librarian has important implications for library education in general.

The Limitations or Failures of Information Services

In the above discussion I have tried to give an overview of some of the more important achievements in the provision of information service in the last few years. Progress has been considerable, but what of the limitations or failures of existing systems? What still needs to be done; in short, what of the future? I would like to give to you some of my own ideas and suggestions on these matters. It is this aspect of my paper that is likely to be more provocative or controversial.

To begin with, I must admit to being diametrically opposed to most of the other speakers at this clinic in one important respect. I firmly believe that if on-line systems are to achieve their true potential in the provision of information service, we must remove the information specialist intermediary and make systems available for use directly by scientists, lawyers, engineers, doctors and other professionals from their own offices, homes or laboratories. The main reason for this statement is my conviction that we must be designing systems to serve a new generation of professionals. This new generation will have grown up with on-line terminals. They will have used on-line terminals as integral tools in the educational process in universities, high schools and even elementary schools. They will have used them in computer-aided instruction, in numerical calculation, and in other applications (e.g., charging out a book from the library).

This new generation of scientists, as well as other professionals, will expect to be able to access bibliographic files through on-line terminal devices. They will use bibliographic systems if terminals are readily available and if the systems are easy to use. There seems little doubt that terminals will be widely available in laboratories, offices, and even in homes. But will our information systems be easy to use?

It seems that we have not given a great deal of consideration to the design of on-line retrieval systems oriented toward use by individuals who are not information specialists. Indeed, as I have pointed out elsewhere, many of the on-line services now in use are former off-line services that have been converted to an on-line mode of access with very few other changes.[8] These off-line systems were designed to be used by information specialists.

Generally, for truly effective use, these systems require fairly extensive training and experience in indexing, in search technique, and in the nuances of a large and sometimes idiosyncratic artificial language in the form of a classification scheme, thesaurus, or list of subject headings. Such systems are designed to be used in a specific search mode. They are not designed with the end user in mind and, by and large, are not suitable for exploitation by the casual (i.e., infrequent) user. In other words, these systems are not user oriented.

Requirements of a User-Oriented System

A user-oriented system must be natural-language oriented. The scientist or other professional will have neither the time nor the inclination to learn the policies, protocols and possible eccentricities associated with human indexing and the use of a large controlled vocabulary. The scientist must be able to interrogate an information system in his own language—the language of scientific discourse, the language of scientific literature, and the language used to communicate with his colleagues.

He probably should be able to interrogate the system by means other than formal searching strategies based on Boolean logic. It may be desirable to allow him to query the system by a natural-language statement, as possible in such systems as SMART, LEADER and BROWSER. These systems are not question-answering systems of the type discussed elsewhere in this volume by Waltz. Rather, they are document or citation retrieval systems that operate essentially by pattern matching—that is, they seek out the documents whose word patterns best match the word pattern of the request for information.

We should also be looking more closely at different approaches to the searching of on-line systems, including searching on the basis of citation indexing and bibliographic coupling. In many retrieval situations, particularly in the sciences, the user does not come to the system knowing nothing about the literature. Indeed, it is quite likely that he is already familiar with some citations to relevant documents. In this situation he should be able to input the relevant citations and simply ask the system to find others like them (e.g., containing similar word patterns or indexed under similar terms).

Keeping convenience to the user in mind at all times, on-line systems should be designed to minimize keyboarding as much as possible. The user should be able to choose from options displayed to him by the system, perhaps (in the case of a video display) by touching the item with a light pen or even a finger. The major system commands should be represented by dedicated keys. Where keyboarding is needed, the system should be reasonably forgiving; it should not be unduly sensitive to minor errors of spelling, punctuation or spacing.

Computers have usually been applied to information retrieval applications in fairly pedestrian ways. They are used mainly as giant matching devices. The innovative applications have come in other fields, such as engineering design and computer-aided instruction. Everyone at this clinic has had the opportunity to see the PLATO system of computer-aided instruction. PLATO has a number of rather unique features including a plasma display, a touch panel, and microfiche and audio interfaces. I believe that the PLATO hardware lends itself to innovative approaches to information retrieval. In one application of PLATO, children can move objects around and put them into containers in order to learn numerical skills. By direct analogy, it should be possible to select terms from displays and place them into "containers" representing various logical search requirements.

Document Delivery

Over the past decade we have provided fairly sophisticated citation retrieval systems, but we have generally neglected the provision of adequate back-up for document delivery. We have created an anomalous situation in which a user might identify citations relevant to some information need in a matter of minutes through an on-line terminal, but might still have to wait several days or even weeks to obtain the documents cited. Clearly, in a really efficient service environment he should be able to obtain the documents in approximately the same time frame in which he finds the citations. A small number of on-line systems, including the New York Times Information Bank, provide rapid document delivery by means of a microfiche interface. It is already technically feasible to transmit microimages to viewing stations over very long distances, but this is still an expensive process.

The whole area of document delivery is one that has been sadly neglected in the design of information services. Most of the major producers of information services are satisfied with producing announcement devices. They either provide no back-up document delivery capability or only a very inadequate one. For the user, the ordering of a document should be as easy as circling a number on an order card. Some industrial information services and a few professional journals (e.g., *Automotive Enginnering*) do make it that easy. *Current Contents* also provides a convenient and rapid document delivery capability. Services of this type, however, should be the rule rather than the exception. A scientist who receives some current awareness mechanism directed to his office should also be able to order documents without leaving his desk. If we are prepared to design personalized current awareness services in which machine listings go directly to a user's office, why do we leave him to his own devices for document delivery purposes, usually requiring him to make a personal visit to the nearest library? In a well designed current awareness service, whether based on a published announcement device or a machine listing, each citation should carry a unique identifying number. The user should be able to order documents from some designated central source simply by circling their numbers on an order card.

Fortunately, the situation in relation to document delivery may be changing. A number of university libraries, including those at Ohio State University and the University of Colorado, have introduced services whereby, in response to a telephone request, library materials are charged out and delivered to faculty offices. An interesting study of the impact of this type of service has recently appeared in a book by Dougherty and Blomquist.[9]

In future on-line information services, at least in certain applications, it will be important to provide document access in approximately the same time frame in which citation access is provided, using stored digital text or a microimage interface. At the very least, it should always be possible to place an order for a document at the on-line terminal. This feature has recently been introduced in connection with on-line access to the NTIS and ISI (Institute for Scientific Information) data bases.

Perhaps the most heartening development on the document delivery scene is the recognition, long overdue, by the major secondary services that the problem is a serious one and that the secondary services have a major responsibility in this area. The recent position statement on document access issued by the National Federation of Abstracting and Indexing Services (NFAIS) identifies the problem very neatly: "The findings of document access studies and the frequent user complaints received by Federation members focus attention on the seriousness of the document access problem. Indeed, member services not directly affiliated with a resource library may be doing themselves, as well as their users, a real disservice by not considering document provision a responsiblity on par with the provision of adequate and accurate abstracts and indexes."[10] The NFAIS statement also proposes a solution to the problem in the shape of a "coordinated document depository system" managed by NFAIS with government support. This is the right idea. Whether or not anything useful comes of it remains to be seen.

Users and User Needs

Many so-called user studies have been conducted by information professionals in the past twenty years. Regrettably, most of these have been a complete waste of time; they have told us nothing we really need to know in order to design new and improved information services. It is my contention that most of the handful of really useful studies have been conducted by sociologists. These are sociometric studies of how information diffuses within a particular community. We as information specialists need to conduct more studies of this kind in order to identify patterns of information flow and to identify the sociometric stars or gatekeepers in various communities. Perhaps the needs of these people should be uppermost in our minds in the design of information services—the people in fact to whom our services should largely be directed, since information directed to them is likely to spread quickly throughout a widespread population.

However excellent large centralized information systems may be, they are unlikely to replace personal information and document files completely. Personal collections are likely to continue; they will still be the first source that the professional turns to when the need for information arises. Personal files have a number of important advantages over central files: they are immediately accessible physically, they contain evaluated items and, perhaps most importantly, they are-indexed in a unique way that represents the user's highly personal viewpoint on the subject matter. We in the information field have tended to overlook the importance of personal files as sources of information. We have done little to encourage the creation of such collections or to help users to organize them. In fact, they have sometimes been discouraged. Assistance in the building and maintenance of personal files would seem, however, to be a legitimate function of the information specialist. Recently, there has been some evidence of interest in this area, as exemplified by a few systems that have been designed specifically to provide on-line support to the personal files of researchers. Such systems include the Remote Information Query System (RIQS) at Northwestern University and the AUTONOTE system at the University of Michigan. I see the need within universities, research institutes, industry, and government agencies for on-line systems that will combine personal files with more general files in a kind of symbiotic relationship. From the same on-line terminal the scientist, or other specialist, would have access to a wide spectrum of information resources: personal files, departmental files, general institutional files (including the library catalog) and finally, various outside data bases of potential value.

Current Awareness Services

A great deal of effort has been spent in the development of so-called current awareness services in the last ten years, as best exemplified, perhaps, by SDI services. In truth, most of these services are not very current at all. Most concentrate on the journal literature, but much of this gets into the great secondary data bases (e.g., *Chemical Abstracts, Biological Abstracts, Index Medicus*) many months after publication. This particular delay, however, is only a minor part of the problem. When an article is published in a scientific journal it is more archival than truly current, since it is likely to appear a year or more after the research reported is completed and perhaps several years after the research project was begun. The scientific journal itself tends to be a very inefficient mechanism for the dissemination of information. It has been pointed out, perhaps first by Herschman,[11] that the scientific journal attempts to undertake three separate and somewhat conflicting functions: an archival function, a social function, and a dissemination function. Many feel that the journal fulfills the first two functions rather well, but the third one rather badly. The scientific journal exists more to serve authors than to serve readers.

Research reported in the journal literature—if it is at the forefront of its field—will have been reported months, perhaps years, earlier at scientific meetings or in the technical report literature. The results of this research will already have been diffused throughout the invisible colleges. Not all will know about the research, but those scientists who are most integrated into the scientific community (who are usually the "key" scientists) will.

Why, then, do we base our current awareness services almost exclusively on the published journal literature, which is not current, and on machine-readable files based on this literature, which are less current still? The only truly *current* current awareness service is one based on ongoing research, disseminating information on research projects before their results are published; the most important example is the Smithsonian Science Information Exchange.

Current awareness services should emphasize ongoing research—and in a sense foster the invisible college phenomenon—making information on "who's doing what" more accessible. A *current* current awareness service should also include references to papers presented at conferences, and those to be presented, and should place more emphasis on the more up-to-date report literature.

Knowledge of Information Sources

We educate librarians and many other information specialists, but why is so little done to educate users of information? A long succession of user studies has revealed that, in virtually all fields studied, there is a general lack of awareness of information resources. A significant proportion of the professional population is not aware of what information services exist in their fields. Many of those who are aware that certain services do exist have little idea of what these services can do for them. Other individuals may use certain information services but not know enough about these to exploit them most effectively.

A recent study among physicians in Toronto, as reported by Woodsworth and Neufeld,[12] is typical of the situation. The physicians surveyed were generally found to lack knowledge of important information services in medicine, including standard printed tools; virtually none had received any formal training in the use of science literature. Yet, and I believe this is highly significant, the majority indicated that they would be interested in attending a seminar or short course on biomedical information retrieval.

Why aren't courses on the use of information resources integrated into university curricula? Within the physics curriculum, for example, there should be one or more courses on information retrieval in physics, covering both published and unpublished sources, including the major information services and centers existing in the field. Similar courses should exist in medicine, agriculture, engineering and other disciplines. A few such courses do exist, mostly in the field of chemistry, but they are few and far between. The education of users of information services has, in general, been sadly neglected. Perhaps this is a legitimate role for schools of library and information science to play. It is certainly a legitimate role for the information services profession. And it is an area that should greatly concern us. We cannot expect people to use information services which they know nothing about.

This brings me to the final point of my paper, a closely related one: the advertising of information services. This is another area that traditionally has been neglected. We tend to be somewhat complacent about the services we provide. In many instances, we seem content to establish some form of information service and then to sit back and wait for users to flock in. Sometimes very little flocking occurs. Perhaps we should concentrate on the sociometric stars—the gatekeepers—to bring our services to the attention of the scientific community. First, however, we must identify these stars and we must be certain that the services we provide are services which are really useful to the professional community—that they are user oriented and convenient to use. We need to apply established techniques of market analysis to determine what services are needed and we must involve users, from the beginning, in the actual design of these services.

This has been a very diffuse paper. It has ranged over many issues and raised a number of questions for which I do not necessarily have the answers. It will have served its purpose if it has encouraged you to look more critically at some of our achievements in the provision of information service. We have made great strides in the last twenty years, but major improvements are still possible and we cannot afford to be complacent about our achievements.

REFERENCES

1. Mooers, Calvin N. "Mooers' Law, or Why Some Retrieval Systems Are Used and Others Are Not," *American Documentation* 11:ii, July 1960.

2. Allen, Thomas J., and Gerstberger, P. G. *Criteria for Selection of an Information Source*. Cambridge, Mass., M. I. T., Sloan School of Management, 1967.

3. Rosenberg, Victor. *The Application of Psychometric Techniques to Determine the Attitudes of Individuals Toward Information Seeking* (Studies in the Man/System Interface in Libraries, Report No. 2). Bethlehem, Pa., Lehigh University, Center for the Information Sciences, 1966.

4. Soper, Mary E. "The Relationship between Personal Collections and the Selection of Cited References." Ph.D. thesis submitted to the University of Illinois Graduate School of Library Science, Urbana, Ill., 1972.

5. Crawford, Susan. "Informal Communication Among Scientists in Sleep Research," *Journal of the American Society for Information Science* 22:301-10, Sept.-Oct.1971.

6. Lancaster, F. W. "A Study of Current Awareness Publications in the Neurosciences," *Journal of Documentation* 30:255-72, Sept. 1974.

7. —————. "The Information Services Librarian," *Australian Special Libraries News* 7:139-49, Nov. 1974.

8. —————. "Can Present Methods for Library and Information Retrieval Services Survive?" *Proceedings of the 1971 Annual Conference of the Association for Computing Machinery*. New York, Association for Computing Machinery, 1971, pp. 564-77.

9. Dougherty, Richard M., and Blomquist, Laura L. *Improving Access to Library Resources*. Metuchen, N. J., Scarecrow Press, 1974.

10. NFAIS Document Access Committee. "NFAIS Position Statement on Document Access, 1975." Philadelphia, National Federation of Abstracting and Indexing Services, Jan. 1975, p. 1.

11. Herschman, Arthur. "The Primary Journal: Past, Present, and Future," *Journal of Chemical Documentation* 10:37-42, Feb. 1970.

12. Woodsworth, Anne, and Neufeld, Victor R. "A Survey of Physician Self-Education Patterns in Toronto. Part 1: Use of Libraries," *Canadian Library Journal* 29:38-44, Jan.-Feb. 1972.

INDEX

Abstracts, searching, 12.

Academic libraries, computer-assisted instruction, 127-35; development of service, 78-90; New York Times Information Bank use, 23; UCLA/ UGA user study, 56-77.

Acquisitions, data base use impact, 7, 14.

American National Standard for Bibliographic Information Interchange on Magnetic Tape, 9.

Australia, data base overview, 111-26.

BASEBALL (natural-language system), 138-39.

Batch systems, Bell Laboratories, 47-50; file structures, 6.

BELDEX (indexing system), 48, 50-51.

Bell Telephone Laboratories, information retrieval methods, 31-55.

Bibliometric research, 42-43.

CA CONDENSATES, compared to Chemical Abstracts, 46-47.

Center for Information Services (CIS) (UCLA), user study, 57-77.

Chemical Abstracts, compared to CA CONDENSATES, 46-47.

Community information centers, 103-10.

Computer-assisted instruction (CAI), 129-35.

Consortium, New York Times Information Bank, 27-29.

Contract negotiation with vendors, NASIC services, 86-87.

Cooperation, impact of automation, 147-48; NASIC, 83-90; New York Times Information Bank use, 27-29.

Costs, academic libraries, 82-83; computer-assisted instruction, 130-31; DIALOG, 39, 41; manual vs. machine searching, 35-36; NASIC, 88-89; New York Times Information Bank, 24-26, 28; processing centers, 13-14.

County records system, 104-08.

Current awareness service, *see* SDI.

Data bases, 3-15.

Demonstrations, *see* promotion of service.

157